UNDERCOVER OPERATOR

UNDERCOVER OPERATOR

WARTIME EXPERIENCES WITH **SOE** IN FRANCE AND THE FAR EAST

SYDNEY HUDSON

LARGE PRINT
Oxford

First published in Great Britain 2003
by
Leo Cooper,
An imprint of Pen & Sword Books Ltd.

Published in Large Print 2005 by ISIS Publishing Ltd.,
7 Centremead, Osney Mead, Oxford OX2 0ES
by arrangement with
Pen & Sword Books Ltd.

British Library Cataloguing in Publication Data
Hudson, Sydney, 1910–
Undercover operator. – Large print ed.
(Isis reminiscence series)
1. Hudson, Sydney, 1910–
2. Great Britain. Special Operations Executive
3. World War, 1939–1945 – Secret service
– Great Britain
4. World War, 1939–1945 – Personal narratives,
British
5. Large type books
I. Title
940.5'48641'092

ISBN 0–7531–9340–X (hb)
ISBN 0–7531–9341–8 (pb)

Printed and bound in Great Britain by
T. J. International Ltd,. Padstow, Cornwall

This book is dedicated to all the brave men and women who risked their lives in the fight against enemy occupation of their countries between 1940 and 1945.

For the morning will come. Brightly will it shine on the brave and true, kindly upon all who suffer for the cause, glorious upon the tombs of heroes. Thus will shine the dawn.

From Winston Churchill's Speech
to the French Nation, 21 October 1940.

Contents

Acknowledgements

I must record my appreciation of the help I have received in the preparation of this book: To my wife for reading the rather illegible manuscript, to Sophie Ayre for turning the manuscript into typescript and to both for many constructive suggestions; to Tom Hartman for his careful editing and to Brigadier Henry Wilson for arranging its publication by Pen & Sword Books Ltd.

Foreword

This book is a personal account of various events leading up to the Second World War, others which occurred during the war, together with a number of incidents which took place after the war but which had a connection with it.

The reader may well ask why I have waited for more than half a century to relate my story. I can only explain that I was involved in various matters totally unconnected with anything that happened during the war and simply never got round to something in the nature of an autobiography. It is only quite recently that I have had sufficient time on my hands. It also seems a pity that some rather interesting events should go untold. Though it is probably the case that my memory of these distant events has necessarily faded, it may also be that I have been able to judge different happenings in a better perspective than if I had been telling my story nearer to the time they took place.

Guide To Code Names And Aliases

The operation in the Sarthe was code-named *Headmaster*.

SOE F Section Personnel

Real Name	Code Name	Code Name in Field	Name in Identity Card
Pierre-Raimond Glaesner	Alcide	Raimond, Kiki	Raimond Perrin
Sonia Butt (d'Artois)	Blanche	Madeleine	Suzanne Bonvie
George Jones	Gaston		
Eugene Bec	Hugue		
Sydney Hudson	Albin	Simon/ Michel	Jacques Laroche, Michel Puisais
Muriel Byck	Michelle	Violette	

The operation in Thailand was code-named *Coupling*.

Our senior Thai organizer was named Snoh Nilkamhaeng, code-named Chew.

I used my real name and code-name Michel and nickname Soapy. Hudson was too much for the Thais who called me Khun (Mr) Sun!

Introduction

When my father was about 22 years old he became ill with TB, or consumption, as it was termed in those days. His worried family despatched him on a round-the-world cruise with stopovers at various places in the Antipodes. Apparently it took him about a year. When he got back his family were alarmed to see that he looked iller than ever. The doctor diagnosed his TB as being in the last stages and informed him that he had six months to live, adding that if he would take a "cure" in Switzerland he might last a year! Opting for a year rather than six months he moved to Arosa — at that time famous for its sanatoria — and at the end of the year — minus one lung — he was cured of TB and subsequently lived to age 73! He decided, nevertheless, to live in Switzerland and met my mother while she was holidaying with her family in Arosa. They were married, I was born and we lived in Montreux where my father's business was centred. Of course everything was interrupted by the outbreak of the First World War in August, 1914. We hurriedly returned to Britain and settled down temporarily in Eastbourne, in a large house belonging to my grandfather. At the age of four I can remember my uncles in army officers' uniform and my aunts as VAD nurses. My mother was head cook in a hospital and my father, unable to pass a medical for active service, worked in a convalescent soldiers' camp.

However, neither of these two latter occupations lasted long as my father, with his knowledge of languages and connections with Switzerland, was posted as a Vice-Consul to the Legation in Montreux. We travelled via Lyon and I well remember seeing an enormous review of French soldiers from our hotel window. It was the spring of 1916 and, I suppose, was intended to be a morale-boosting exercise. The losses on the Western front were piling up and the population was already under pressure.

Everything seemed relatively peaceful in Switzerland. True, food was apparently rationed, but at the age of six this was the least of my worries! There were quite a number of Allied soldiers who had been wounded and, by international agreement, interned in the French-speaking canton of Vaud. Among them was a Belgian cousin of my family who had been badly wounded in the head and lost an eye. He was a jolly person, in spite of his injuries, and after the war became a monk.

I was given French lessons and, playing with Swiss children, soon began to converse happily with them. After about a year in Montreux my father was transferred to St Gallen in German Switzerland where his duties involved reading the newspapers printed in Germany and questioning persons who had come from that country. All with a view to gleaning any information which might be useful to the British Intelligence services operating through the Legation in Berne.

Shortly after arriving in St Gallen I contributed to my parents' other worries by becoming extremely ill with bronchitis. When I finally recovered it was in a somewhat enfeebled state and the doctor considered that mountain air would be good for me. My mother and I were installed at father's one-time place of cure — Arosa. We stayed there until the end of the war. Of course, because the area was German-speaking the interned, wounded prisoners of war were German. They were in uniform and we looked at them rather askance, but they seemed harmless enough!

Our stay in Arosa was uneventful enough except for one curious personal psychological phenomenon. I was now eight years old and was, I suppose, externally fairly normal. Unknown to my parents, perhaps related to my spell of bronchitis, I had two secret terrors. One was that mountains neighbouring Arosa would fall on us — they were actually miles away. My other terror was that the hotel in which we lived would go on fire. Both these terrors, unspoken but real enough to me, vanished completely when we left Arosa at the end of the war.

It was May 1919. My father's job as Vice-Consul had come to an end; he had become a correspondent of the *Morning Post* and had also set up an English language "weekly" — *The English Herald Abroad*. His office was in Montreux. There was a considerable number of Britons living in Switzerland in those days. They had their own grocer, Mr Whitely, and their own tailor, Mr Moore. I can remember the latter providing me with a plus-four suit — very smart and typically British.

We lived in Villars-sur-Ollon. From there my father could easily commute to Montreux and it provided a marvellous Alpine environment. We lived contentedly there for two decades. It was a particularly good place for summer and winter sports. I played golf and tennis in the summer with occasional interludes for mountain climbing. In the winter I skied and played ice hockey. All of this obviously left me little time for any educational studies!

During all these years I was subject to two contrasting influences. My family was British and we spoke English at home and I was brought up with English history and literature. Once out of the house, however, my environment was totally French-speaking except for a couple of months of the year. In December the British arrived for the winter sports. For a few weeks I became quite friendly with some of them but of course they went home when their holidays were over.

When I was about 18 years of age my father started to develop an agency for importing British goods into Switzerland. I joined him in this and I gradually became quite interested in the business.

In summary I can say I was bi-lingual, was friendly with people from many walks of life but had no real friends. Sometimes this saddened me a little when I thought of it. In time I grew accustomed to a situation which made me something of a "loner".

CHAPTER ONE

Into War

Like many other boys brought up in the inter-war years I was educated, implicitly and at times explicitly, to admire two conflicting ideals. Of course my parents and teachers were not to know that one day these ideals would confront the more philosophically minded members of my generation with a rather stark choice.

On the one hand, we were presented with the ideal of the pacifist, suffering hero, predominantly, but not totally Christian. Such were Jesus himself, Socrates and Thomas More, to name but three. By contrast with them stood such famous warriors as Richard Coeur de Lion, Henry V and Wellington, together with the soldiers of the Great War. The latter had, so it was thought, fought "the War to end Wars", which set them in a class apart.

For quite a few years these two ideals were in contrast but hardly in a mind-splitting conflict. We read in the newspapers that in a University debating society the students had voted that in any future war they "would not fight for King and Country". Most of us, however, were supremely unconcerned.

For me the atmosphere began to change in 1936. It was the year of the Winter Olympic Games at Garmisch Partenkirchen and I had the doubtful honour of being a member of the British Ski Team. I say doubtful as I ran into a tree in the first 50 metres of the downhill race and certainly got no honour at all! It was the opening ceremony which gave cause for thought: cheering crowds and the teams all saluting the Führer of the German Reich, Adolf Hitler! Well, we pretended that it was the Olympic salute, not the Nazi one, but for the crowd it made no difference. It was the raised arm that was important — and how they cheered.

During the years that followed I married and worked in the family business in Switzerland. We had an office in Lutry near Lausanne and specialized in distributing various chemicals on behalf of I.C.I. I counted myself as something of an expert in descaling boilers and pipelines. When I had time to think about it (I continued to ski in the winter and to play a lot of golf in the summer), I could see that the world situation was growing ever more menacing. Much outrage was caused in Switzerland by the German publication of a map which purported to show the new Germany, entitled the Third Reich, whose frontiers enveloped the whole of German-speaking Switzerland.

About the time of the Munich crisis in 1938 an incident occurred which affected me considerably. Some Jewish acquaintances of my family had emigrated to Switzerland. I knew of course that the Nazis had persecuted the Jews since they came to power in 1933, but, though I felt an uneasy distaste for what was going on, I had no personal contact with it. Now it was different. The acquaintances — a man and his wife — had been living undisturbed near Lausanne on a visitor's visa which they apparently had no particular difficulty in obtaining. When the time came for the visa to be renewed they were dismayed to find that the Swiss authorities absolutely refused to do so. Various persons, including members of my family, were asked to contact the Bureau des Etrangers, but to no avail. The Swiss authorities were impervious to argument. Herr and Frau Wärendorf, as they were called, must leave the country immediately. To go back to Germany would mean imprisonment or forced labour. They were unable to obtain a French visa either. In total desperation, they attempted to cross the frontier into France illegally. Of course they were arrested by the French Police and imprisoned in Annenasse. We heard they were befriended by a local Jewish businessman and, much later, that somehow they had managed to reach Britain. The fact that an apparently harmless middle-aged couple could be driven from their home to seek safety in Switzerland and that Switzerland — the traditional refuge of the persecuted of all lands — had chosen to expel them, presumably under pressure from the Nazis, was a dramatic reality. It was distinct from the reports and articles which were appearing in the newspapers at the time which one tended to regard as exaggerated, and struck me with a sense of foreboding which I had not felt before.

No need to enumerate the fateful landmarks of the years that led up to the war, culminating in the Munich capitulation. The clouds darkened with every month, yet I managed to work in the chemicals business, whilst continuing to ski and play golf, oblivious to the doom-laden events which were impending in 1939. The Swiss Open Championship took place at the end of August at Crans sur Sierre and I was remarkably satisfied with myself for taking the first amateur prize. On arriving home I found my family making hasty arrangements to leave Switzerland within the next three or four days. War was evidently about to be declared. All my interests had collapsed and to add insult to injury the Swiss Army served notice that my car was to be requisitioned immediately!

On arriving in Britain, it was evident that everybody had made up their minds that war with Germany was inevitable. We all settled down with my aunt who occupied, alone, a rambling old manor house not far from Eastbourne. Thanks to my aunt, who was an Alderman of the Town Council, I found myself volunteering for any kind of local job. So it was that I joined a team zealously occupied in sandbagging the municipal rubbish destructor — although it seemed doubtful if the German bombers would select it as their target. The remainder of my time was spent in collecting petrol, prior to the imminent introduction of rationing. I stored it in every container I could find, many of them open! It was a good thing none of us smoked! On 3 September 1939 at 11 o'clock Neville Chamberlain, the man who only a year before had ecstatically informed us that it was "peace for our time" now stated that we were "at war with Germany". Those of us who, for lack of a better term, were ethically minded were now presented with the starkest possible choice. We would have to become involved in the war or declare ourselves conscientious objectors. From an ethical point of view "being involved in the war" meant anything from work in a munitions factory to fighting with bayonets and hand grenades. Where were the great religions and philosophies in all this? "Turn the other cheek", "Treat all men as brothers", "Have compassion for all living creatures", "Campaign in the method of non-violence" and how many other injunctions urging, indeed commanding, us not to go to war? Doubtless in every war that was ever fought men have thought that theirs was the righteous cause. But who could doubt that Hitler and the Nazis were evil? The persecution of the Jews and the evidence of the *Kristallnacht*, the invasion of Czechoslovakia and now of Poland showed that their ambition was none other than world domination. "Turning the other cheek" would be simply to accept subjugation. Clearly, one would have either to find some occupation such as cultivating cabbages or becoming a front line soldier or an air force pilot. It was of course obvious that conscription would eventually catch up with all the adult population — so volunteering would probably enable one to choose one's wartime career!

With thoughts such as these I proceeded to the local H.Q. of the Territorial Army in Hastings. To my surprise I was informed that the Army was not prepared at the time to recruit anyone and that all applicants for the Services would have to wait for an indefinite period — almost certainly several months.

In the interim I went into a small factory, in which my father had an interest. It was manufacturing electrical measuring equipment for the Services and I took over the stores and purchasing department. I quickly found out how very many parts went into instruments of this type. Any one of these, which I might forget to order, could throw the whole sequence of the production line into disarray. It was quite an experience!

I heard nothing of the Army through all the winter of 1939–40. It was the period of the "phoney war" and, having once committed myself to Army service, I felt rather indignant at not being accepted immediately! However, a war *was* going on and a very real one at that. It was the time when the Soviet Union had invaded Finland and the Finns were struggling desperately and at times quite successfully against far more powerful forces. I heard vaguely that the Finns were trying to recruit British volunteers to add support for their Army. I thought, with my new-found zeal for action, that this might be just the thing for me — after all the Soviet Union was the Ally of Germany (these were the days of the Ribbentrop — Molotov non-aggression pact) so that by helping the Finns I would indirectly be having a go at Germany as well. It would be in accordance with my idealism and of course the Finnish Army was fighting part of its war on skis. Not quite the downhill skiing to which I had been accustomed in Switzerland perhaps, but surely I would be able to adapt well into the Finnish winter campaigns?

With these ideas I presented myself to the Finnish Embassy. The staff were quite welcoming. They sent me for medical examination which I passed and was impatiently awaiting call-up and transportation to Finland. It all came to nothing. In the spring of 1940 the Russians broke through the Mannerheim line, threatened Helsinki and the Finns were forced to capitulate. I kept on with my job in Measuring Instruments (Pullin) as the company was called. At Easter we were intending to close down the factory and all the staff were planning to devote themselves to family or sport or a mixture of the two!

Suddenly the nation was shaken out of its almost trance-like passivity by the news that Germany had invaded Denmark and Norway. The Easter holiday was forgotten and a new atmosphere of apprehension combined with a certain thrill pervaded all our doings.

Shortly afterwards it appeared that recruitment to the Services was now open. I left my job, visited my relations and started to try and get physically fit. It was the time of Dunkirk and the collapse of the French Army. Now the German panzers had penetrated to the mouth of the Somme, cutting the Allied front in two. They had attempted to do this for the whole of the 1914–18 War and in the end had been totally defeated. Now the victory in the "War to end Wars" was shown to have been nothing but a myth.

In the first week of May I presented myself to the recruiting station in Acton. The kindly officer in charge asked, as I was a volunteer, what I would like to join. "The infantry," I said, quickly adding "Sir."

"What regiment?" I had no idea.

"The Royal Fusiliers is a very good regiment," the officer affirmed paternally. So it was that on 13 June 1940, when the world that we had known was falling in ruins about us, I reported to the Hounslow Barracks of the Royal Fusiliers.

The Hendon Drill Hall was where the intake of some three hundred recruits to the Royal Fusiliers was housed, fed and trained. I will not go into my experiences of this period, as they must have been more or less identical with those of the millions of men who were being drafted in to the Services in the war years. Suffice it to say that the world shrank to the limits of presenting oneself to Sergeant's inspection, drilling, exercising, marching, eating and sleeping. Now and again news penetrated through the mist — most alarmingly the capitulation of France and the installation of the Vichy government with Marshal Pétain at its head.

I felt this as something of a body blow. I thought of my French friends and the places I knew, the mountains, the towns, the wonderful cathedrals and churches, the long straight roads through the fields and forests — all now under the control of the hated Boches. Pétain would surely be a façade for the German occupation. With thoughts such as these I sat in the NAAFI, munching some chocolate and drinking a bottle of orangeade. The food which the Royal

Fusiliers provided for the recruits was totally inedible and we relied on our families or a restaurant for an evening meal. We were allowed out of barracks on most days of the week.

Then came the Battle of Britain and the Blitz on London. From Hounslow we could see the orange glow in the sky and as many of us had families and friends in the city, a dull and continuous anxiety was the background to our strenuous training programme. One afternoon in late October, together with one of my fellow Fusiliers, we decided to see what London in the bombing was like. We took the District Line to Whitechapel and then walked through the East End towards Bethnal Green. Dusk was falling and the streets in the blackout were almost deserted. The effects of the bombing were everywhere to see — shattered houses, streets blocked either with heaps of rubble or cordoned off with the notice "unexploded bomb". By the time we got back in to the Tube people were beginning to crowd the platforms, camping there for the night. We were becoming increasingly worried at the time spent in moving from one place to another. We had to be at Hammersmith Station at 11 o'clock to join another friend who would give us a lift by car back to Hounslow and be at the Drill Hall by 12 o'clock. Failure to report in by midnight would be certain to earn us a black mark which would count against our possible transfer to an officers' training corps at the end of our four months' basic training. At the Strand station at about half-past ten, the platforms choked with people tucking themselves up for the night, the trains came to a total stop. We made our way towards the escalator, avoiding the stretched-out bodies and finally emerged into the Strand. The whole street was empty and, of course, completely dark — there was the sound of bombs exploding not very far away. Walking to Hammersmith would probably take about three hours we reckoned and by then our friend would long have given us up. Suddenly while we were already contemplating the slating the Sergeant Major would give us, together with the prospect of the "black mark" condemning us to the ranks indefinitely, a taxi came down the Strand, its little blue light showing that it was free. We hailed it and the driver, apparently indifferent to bombs and blackout, drove us with complete assurance to Hammersmith station where our "pick-up" was waiting. By midnight we had checked in to the guardroom and proceeded peacefully to bed.

On one occasion, a Sunday, a day on which we were free of military duties, I agreed with one of my fellow Fusiliers that we would play golf. He was a member of the Roehampton G.C. and was also the owner of a car. My wife was staying with her aunt in the country at the time and the flat in which we had been living near Earls Court was unoccupied. We passed that way before going to Roehampton in order to collect my golf clubs. When we reached the street in Earls Court there was a barrier across it and a notice in large letters which read "No Entry. Unexploded Bomb"! We knew, of course, that there had been a raid on London the night before but Earls Court seemed a bit far from the centre of town. Well, anyway, here it was. I was certainly not going to let my clubs be blown up or indeed to have our prospective game spoiled. The street was deserted. I went to the house in which our flat was; nobody was there and everything seemed undamaged. I unlocked the door, fetched my golf clubs, closed it again and then walked down the street, rather quickly, to where my friend was waiting. We had a nice game at Roehampton. Looking up to the sky we could see vapour trails all over it. There seemed to be some kind of aerial battle going on. In the evening we returned to the Hendon Drill Hall.

At the end of our recruit training at Hendon I was placed in a group selected to go on Officer Training. This was to take place in the Isle of Man and under considerably more comfortable circumstances than in the strict discipline of the Hendon Drill Hall. The course lasted for three months and at the end I was proudly commissioned as a Second Lieutenant in the Royal Fusiliers — collar, tie and all.

I joined a battalion which was assigned to guarding the South Downs against a German parachute attack. I have to say that I was bored stiff. One event, however, stands out in my memory. I was sleeping at the time in the Stewards' Stand at Lewes Racecourse — ready for the parachutists of course — when I woke to a horrible smell. Whilst I was wondering whether the batmen had burned our breakfast, someone hammered on the window and told me to get out at top speed — the house was on fire! So it was and I only got out just in time!

It was not long after that a friend was able to obtain my transfer to an organization with the name of Auxiliary Units. This consisted of specially selected men of the Home Guard led by Army officers who were to operate, in the event of a German invasion, behind the enemy lines. To this end carefully camouflaged hideaways, each capable of holding about seven men, were scattered over the south-east of England. The officer in charge of a given area, comprising some six to eight hideaways and consequently around fifty men, was responsible for field and weapons training and in the storage of ammunition, explosives and three weeks' supply of food. During the summer and autumn of 1941 the H.Q. for East Kent was situated near Ashford. There was a neighbouring forest admirably suited for practising guerrilla warfare. On days when our patrols were not training I was allocated a car and supervised the work going on at the hideaways. What fun it all was — until it dawned on me that the anticipated German landings were becoming less likely by the day. Hitler seemed to be fully occupied on the Russian front and would surely be unable to mount the military effort it would need to attempt the invasion of Britain.

In December 1941 I went on a one-week course at the central H.Q. of the Auxiliary Units near Swindon. All the participants were given an interview with the Commanding Officer on the final day. In mine I thought to mention that I had a pretty good knowledge of French which, with appropriate modesty, I suggested might be useful. He told me to put the matter in a letter. As it happened this was to be the turning point of my whole life. However, at the time, on returning to Ashford, I only felt somewhat annoyed at discovering that I had left all my blankets behind at Swindon H.Q.! I thought that somehow my equipment roll felt lighter! I duly wrote the letter which the C.O. had suggested. It was couched in the appropriate Army language ending, "I have the honour to be, Sir, your obedient servant" and simply repeated what I had said about the possible usefulness of my knowledge of French.

Shortly after the New Year I received a curt formal note from the War Office (no less!) ordering me to report there the following week on a fixed day and time. In service dress with brass buttons and belt buckle well shined, I presented myself at the military holy of holies. A messenger, first checking my identity, took me to Room 505. A friendly looking Major rose from his desk and told me to sit down. He held the formal letter which I had written to the C.O. of the Auxiliary Units. He then asked me a number of questions relating to my pre-war past. He spoke for a short time in French and appeared satisfied with my linguistic ability. Then he came to the point: I was to be parachuted into France to organize resistance groups and train them to attack and sabotage the German lines of communication against the day which would one day come when there would be a front line in mainland Europe. There would be a prolonged training period. He ended by remarking cheerfully that normally he left interviewees to consider the matter but that in my case, as I had volunteered already, this was obviously unnecessary. In fact, I had simply stated in my letter that I thought my knowledge of French might be useful without any idea in what it would involve me. However, I could see that I was committed now anyway. This would surely be in line with my original thinking that if one was not going to be a conscientious objector one should be "up front" in the war. This looked as though it would certainly be all of that. In any case, it would be a change from the boring procedures and discipline of the Army.

Major Gielgud (he was a cousin of the famous actor John Gielgud) shook hands and a messenger showed me out into the street. I walked slowly up Whitehall and across Trafalgar Square. I kept thinking to myself, "This is serious now", in a curious mood of self-importance combined with a certain apprehension. On the corner by the National Portrait Gallery there stands a statue of Edith Cavell. I went over to it. It commemorates the deeds of Nurse Cavell in helping British soldiers to escape during the German occupation of Brussels in the Great War. "Shot at dawn" reads the inscription — a telling example to those fighting the war not in uniform. There was a further inscription: "Patriotism is not enough," she had said. I stepped back and saluted. I had ample cause for thought as I sat down to a cup of tea and a poached egg on toast at a Lyons Corner House.

It was not long before I received a note ordering me to report to the War Office again with all my equipment. Thence I was told to proceed to No. 5 Orchard Court by taxi. I found it to be a flat with a civilian in charge. To meet me was a Captain wearing

General Services badges. In a friendly way he informed me that I was to go to Guildford where I would be met and taken to a Special Training School where I would be likely to be for three weeks. He added that my name would now be Hill! It sounded rather mysterious and exciting.

At the STS I found myself in a group of some twenty individuals very different from those whom I had enountered in the Royal Fusiliers or in Auxiliary units. They were all, or nearly all, French-speaking Britons. I discovered later that French nationals were recruited into a separate organization under General de Gaulle, it having apparently been agreed with the General that the organization to which I now belonged, entitled F Section, Special Operation Excecutive (SOE), would consist of non-French. This obviouly placed "the Firm", as we called SOE, in a situation of considerable difficulty. To staff its undercover operations would need men and, later in the war, women, who were able to pass as native French citizens. This obviously excluded all the young men who were at that time volunteering for duties which carried a particular level of risk, e.g. RAF flying personnel, commandos, submarine crews, paratroopers etc. In addition, they would have to assimilate with the general population. Six and a half-foot Vikings would definitely not qualify as members of the Firm's F Section. For the Norwegian Section, provided of course that they spoke Norwegian as natives, they would probably have been most welcome.

As I got to know my particular group better, it was easy to see, although we were all instructed to say as little as possible about our personal histories, that we were from the most varied backgrounds imaginable. I recall especially two brothers who were professional acrobats, one commercial artist and one mirror maker. (He mentioned with some pride that he was expert in preparing see-through mirrors which fetched a good price for persons wishing to see into their visitors' bathroom!)

The motivations of this curious group of French-speaking Britons seemed to have one thing in common. Because they had mainly been brought up in France and, in addition to the language, their background, culture and education had been essentially French, now, with the collapse of France and the emergence of the Vichy government, they were keen to demonstrate that they were indeed British. Certainly their determination was not to be doubted.

The first three weeks of our training were mostly devoted on how to live clandestinely. The use of false identities, the sabotage of equipment essential to the enemy, the handling of explosives and weapons comprised our programme. In my case one unexpected problem revealed itself in talking to my new friends. My French, although I was more or less bilingual, had a noticeable Swiss accent! During the months that followed I worked hard to eliminate this and, according to my fellow course members, more or less succeeded.

Following the three weeks at the Guildford STS it was evident that a few members of the group had been eliminated — we never knew why! Our next stage was near Loch Morar in the very depths of the Scottish Highlands. What a time we had! Especially me — climbing in the hills, rock climbing, shooting with various weapons, demolitions, pretending to sabotage the railway from Fort William to Mallaig. Only occasionally did the thought occur to us that, perhaps in the rather near future, all this might be for real! Moving from Scotland to Manchester reality seemed a step closer when we undertook our parachute course at Ringway aerodrome. After a few sessions involving jumping through holes and rolling over on coconut matting, we were taken up for our first real jump. This was quite an experience; first the nervous tension (not frightened of course!) and then the feeling of exhilaration as one floats down under the opened canopy. The fourth jump was scheduled to be at night from a balloon. We were warned that this involved a rather disagreeable pause before the chute opened. As luck would have it the weather was bad when our turn came and we were due to go on leave the next day. The Captain in charge of training asked if we were sufficiently confident to forego the fourth jump. We assured him that we were. Doubtfully he asked us if we would not like to stay on for a day or two giving time for the weather to clear. We thanked him but declined his kind offer!

Two other courses followed, one in the techniques of underground warfare and another on industrial sabotage. In connection with our instruction on how to damage or destroy machinery, railway engines, electrical plant, etc, it is amusing to recall some of the fantastic ideas which the assorted boffins had thought up. In the course of time, the veil of secrecy has been lifted on some of these "dirty tricks" as they were called: exploding rats, camel dung concealing a charge, booby traps of all kinds. Then there was a possibility that agents might be traced by using dogs to sniff out their hideouts. Bitches' urine might be the answer. Surely that would put any dog off the trail. But then suppose the Germans would pursue us with bitches? Eureka, if we put bears' fat on our shoes that would just scare the life out of any dog, male or female. A designated boffin, it was said, actually got in touch with London Zoo. Sadly, the Zoo did not want to part with its bears, which on their wartime diet were a trifle thin anyway! I think the champion of the boffin's ideas was to provide SOE's agents with tins of a particular kind of insect (I've forgotten its name) which afflict cattle. The insects lay their eggs in the cattle hide and the larvae eat it. Then, when the German army needed leather for the boots of its soldiers it would be full of holes. They would probably have to stop the war!

Then we were ready for our final test. (This test became more fearsome in later years, including a mock arrest and subsequent interrogation.) My task was to reconnoitre the Manchester Ship Canal with a view to planning sabotage. It involved living incognito with false papers. My cover story was to walk along the bank taking samples of the water. I decided on one of the bridges. The bridge keeper was most helpful, allowing me to go underneath the bridge (to sample the water!).

I wrote a report on the reconnaissance which seemed to satisfy the authorities. I hope it didn't get the bridge keeper into trouble.

During the training period we had had two or three interviews with the Commanding Officer of F Section — Major, later Colonel, Buckmaster. He decided that my operational area would be the Auvergne as I knew it quite well from holidays spent at Le Mont-Doré. It was a little disappointing I thought not to be assigned to the so-called Occupied Zone, where the Germans were in total control. In the Free Zone the Vichy government, though obedient to the Germans, were ostensibly in charge.

We were to be a team of three — two agents and one radio operator. The training courses had brought us together so that we knew each other quite well. During our last leave in August 1942 we took a week to "toughen ourselves up" in Wales, scrambling up Snowdon in the process. The other agent was Brian Rafferty and the radio operator George Jones.

We were given a careful briefing by Maurice Buckmaster and his two deputies, Jerry Morell and Vera Atkins. This included issuing identity cards and accompanying cover stories and a safe house where we were to proceed from the area into which we had been parachuted. Our landing ground was to be south of Clermont Ferrand and, if all went well, the "safe house" address was given as Monsieur Néraud, 37 Rue Blatin, Clermont Ferrand. Jerry Morell, who had some experience of Vichy France, encouragingly remarked that if we were caught by the French police in time they would always let us go!

On 23 September I travelled up to Shrewsbury to see my daughter who had been born the day before. Everything seemed to be satisfactory and I returned to Paddington station late in the evening. The roof of the station had been completely blown off and a brilliant moon shone through. The following morning I met up at Orchard Court with Brian (codenamed Michel) and George (codenamed Gaston). Maurice Buckmaster and Vera Atkins were there to wish us good luck and we got into a staff car and drove to a stately home (yet another!) serving the Tempsford aerodrome. We were then given a thorough check to make sure that nothing incriminating might be in our pockets or in our — rather modest — belongings. We were then issued with our parachute equipment. Finally came dinner with a bottle of wine and a rather forced jollity. At about 9 o'clock a car arrived to take us to the aerodrome. Our plane was standing on the tarmac and, with a quick handshake to our guide, we got on and the door was shut.

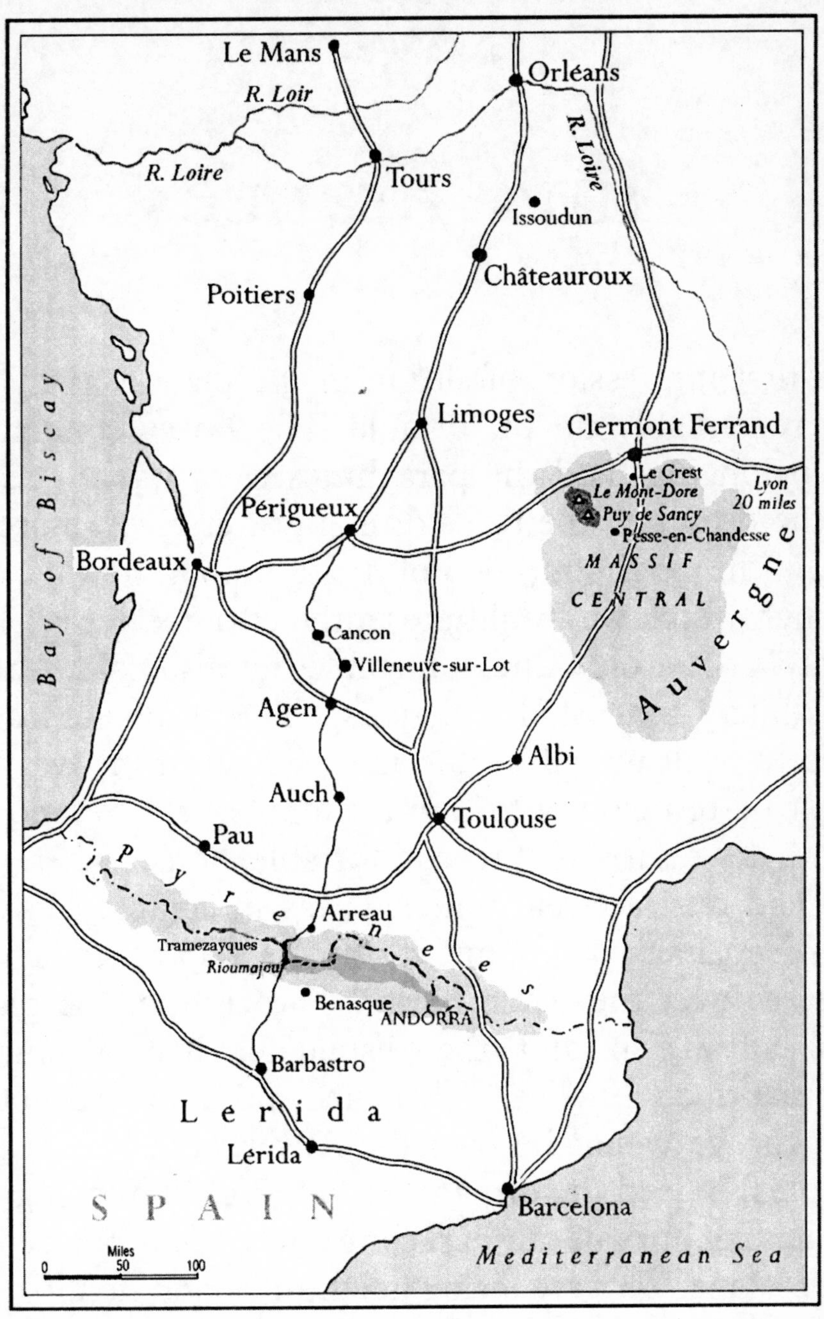
Le Mans
Orléans
R. Loir
R. Loire
R. Loire
Tours
Issoudun
Châteauroux
Poitiers
Bay of Biscay
Limoges
Clermont Ferrand
Le Crest
Le Mont-Dore
Puy de Sancy
Lyon 20 miles
Pesse-en-Chandesse
MASSIF CENTRAL
Auvergne
Périgueux
Bordeaux
Cancon
Villeneuve-sur-Lot
Agen
Albi
Auch
Toulouse
Pau
Pyrenees
Arreau
Tramezayques
Rioumajou
Benasque
ANDORRA
Barbastro
Lerida
Lerida
SPAIN
Barcelona
Mediterranean Sea
Miles
0 50 100

CHAPTER TWO

Into France

The first impression of sitting in the plane was that it was remarkably uncomfortable. The boxes containing our belongings and the parachutes were stacked ready for the drop and the three of us put ourselves, more or less, in the neighbourhood of the trap door, now closed, through which we would presently let ourselves go. The flight was not only uncomfortable but also cold. Above the dulling roar of the engines, the tension increased steadily. I felt myself wondering whether, if the weather might be too cloudy to find a suitable field to land in, we might return to the comfortable house where we had had our farewell dinner. I was interrupted in this half-sleep, half-wishful musing by the dispatcher saying, "We are over the River Loire." The crew of the plane were all Polish and the dispatcher had a limited command of English. What he said now was clear enough. We would be over the Auvergne in just a few minutes. Indeed the dispatcher was already hitching the connecting lines of our parachutes to a rail in the centre of the plane. We were losing height now and he took the cover off the hole in the floor. We could vaguely see the hills and forests below. Brian put his legs in the hole, a red light overhead turned to green, the dispatcher shouted "Go," and he instantly disappeared. George was next and again the dispatcher shouted, "Go." Then it was my turn. We had been trained to the point of having a conditioned reflex to the word "Go" and almost before I knew it I was in the buffeting slipstream of the plane. I felt the tug of the connecting line and in a few seconds the canopy of the parachute opened above me. For a moment a glorious sense of exhilaration overcame me; I could see the mountains of the Auvergne, black against the moonlit sky.

The exhilaration was short-lived. I could see that we had been dropped from far too high and that my companions and the other parachutes with the packages containing the radio set and all our equipment and clothes were drifting further and further apart. I lost sight of almost all of them when I suddenly saw the ground coming up to meet me! I landed gently enough, folded up my parachute and then began to look for my companions and the packages. I soon met up with George, who had narrowly missed falling into a vineyard where the staked vines would have made for a particularly unpleasant landing! We located the package containing the radio and one other. Two were missing. Of Brian there was no sign. We buried our parachutes, our revolvers and overalls. We then tried to locate Brian and the remaining packages. As dawn broke we found one of the packages. We saw that we were in a landscape of fields and vineyards. There was no one in sight. We hid the packages we had found and searched all day for the others, which, in addition to very useful personal belongings, contained some documents relating to our false identities. At nightfall we abandoned the search, collected a large amount of delicious grapes from the vineyards and lay down in a kind of workman's shack. At earliest light, fortified by a ration of amphetamine pills, we made our way, following a map, to the town of Clermont Ferrand. A rough path led over some hills then broadened out into a road and finally into a street. We were going, maybe, for some four or five hours. Curiously, on the gateway of a house in the outer suburbs of the town was a graffito in large blue letters which read, *"La Mort du Boche, approche."* It seemed rather encouraging! We had still seen nothing of Brian but were not unduly worried as he had the same "safe-house" rendezvous as we had.

We entered the Place Jean Jaurès, I remembered it from holidays long ago. Everything appeared to be exactly the same. The local cinema, incredibly, was playing *The Hunchback of Notre Dame*; starring Charles Laughton! Nobody took any notice of us whatever. We soon found 37 Rue Blatin. A card beside the door showed this to be the residence of Monsieur and Madame Néraud. Ringing the bell we entered and were welcomed as old friends. Yes, Brian had called the day before and had been passed on to another "safe house" in the country. We were introduced to two young men — Roger and Maurice Werther. They were to take us to the village of Le Crest about 15kms from Clermont Ferrand where we could easily be housed in one of the old semi-deserted farmhouses. There were many such in the countryside neighbouring Clermont Ferrand. The agricultural population had quitted their traditional way of life to work in factories — notably in the Michelin Tyre plant.

We walked separately so as not to attract too much notice and, with the help of another amphetamine tablet, I reached Le Crest in about four hours and easily found the house. We were introduced to Madame Werther, mother of the two young men. The Werthers were Jews, their father had been gassed in the Great War and had died some time in the 1920s. Roger and his mother had kept a shop in the Passy district of Paris while Maurice was a "professeur" in a lycée. Madame Werther was rather elderly, somewhat bent and a lady of great determination.

We ate bread and cheese and drank coffee made of ground-up acorns! We discussed the situation in France and possible plans for future operations. George and the Werther brothers smoked and smoked! We had brought six packets of cigarettes with us and in two hours they were all finished!

The Werthers reported that the French attitude to the war was now changing considerably. Immediately after the armistice there was a sense of relief, particularly of course in the so-called *Zone Libre*, Marshal Pétain having miraculously negotiated a peace treaty with Hitler. The French prisoners of war would be set free and life would return to its pre-war pleasantness. The Werthers, as Jews, did not return to Paris and apparently had nothing to fear in the *Zone Libre*. Britain was almost an enemy — witness the destruction of the French fleet at Oran — and would, in any case, soon fall to a German invasion.

The situation was different by the early autumn of 1942. Britain had not been invaded, the Germans were engaged on the Russian front and the United States had entered the war. In such circumstances public opinion was hardening in favour of the Allies. Probably the most important factor was the fate of the prisoners of war who, instead of the expected return home, were constrained to work in German factories and as farm labourers in replacement of the men who had been called up.

We decided to place George and his radio set in the house of a friend of the Werthers some distance from Le Crest. The two brothers and I set off on a walking tour to prospect for landing grounds for parachute drops. It was a remarkably pleasant experience. All the feeling of danger had already disappeared. We took a bus to Besse-en-Chandesse and scrambled up to the summit of the Puy de Sancy, the highest point of the Auvergne. (I think I can claim to be the only person to have climbed both Snowdon and the Sancy in 1942!) We descended, via the Mont-Doré. I briefly considered whether I would contact the proprietors of the Hotel des Étrangers where I had stayed before the war. They would be useful as members of our future organization, but might well be supporters of the Vichy régime. Too dangerous, I thought. We pitched camp on the fringes of the one-time golf course. Next morning we proceeded via the rather spectacular Roche Sanadoire to a high plateau without any habitations or roads and which could not be overlooked — an ideal place for parachuting men or packages of weapons and explosives. We stayed one night in a country inn in Zanières. The owner was again a friend of the Werthers and George was installed there with his radio set. We returned the following day to Le Crest.

The next day or two passed uneventfully enough. One morning, I think it was 8 October, when we returned to the Werthers' house after splitting logs for the cooking stove, we noticed a black Citroën car outside the door. The brothers told me that they thought it belonged to a relation of their neighbour who occasionally came to visit him. We walked into the living room and immediately encountered two men who informed us that they were police inspectors and that the three of us were under arrest.

They searched the house and quickly identified as suspicious the clasp knife which was issued by SOE to parachute personnel. It was not marked by any sign but the police must have found other ones earlier as part of other agents' belongings. The senior police officer, we subsequently found out that his name was Trotta, told us we could eat something while they continued their search; afterwards we would be taken to Clermont Ferrand. After a rather desultory piece of bread and cheese given us by Madame Werther, the two brothers and me were ordered into the back of the black Citroën and, with the two police officers in front, we set off. I briefly considered jumping on them from behind but, in the first place thought that it might simply provoke a serious accident, but secondly I had a feeling that the police must surely be on our side. I recalled that in our briefing we had been told that in due course they would let any agents they captured escape. With these thoughts we arrived at the main police station, were separated and I, at least, was subjected to rigorous interrogation.

At first I stuck to my carefully prepared cover story. I was from Paris; the address was 87 Rue de Faisanderie. I had just crossed into the *Zone Libre* and was staying with the Werther family whom I had known in Paris. I gave various references — more or less distinguished. "Was I Jewish perhaps?" "No, certainly not." I had left Paris because I had thought life would be easier in the *Zone Libre* and food more plentiful in the countryside. The police officers — the two who had arrested us had been joined by an older, apparently more senior man — now carefully inspected my identity card which had been given me in my London briefing. It purported to have been issued by the Préfecture de la Seine, the idea being that it would be next to impossible to trace it from the *Zone Libre*. I felt that so far my story had held up rather convincingly, so I felt all the more shock when the senior officer, almost casually, remarked, "Now perhaps you had better tell us how it comes that you are in possession of a forged identity card."

"Forged?" I said with determined indignation. "It was issued to me by the Préfecture de la Seine."

"Anyone can see that it is forged," said the man, rather impatiently. "Amongst other things, the thumb print is imposed in a way totally different from the way they do it at the Préfecture. In addition, a package with its parachute attached was picked up the other day about 20kms south of here and as we have a clasp-knife of yours of a type that we have connected with parachutists before you might as well tell us all about it. We know the Werther family are your accomplices."

Faced with this situation, I thought as rapidly as I could. In our briefing we had been told that if our cover stories had been totally blown there was nothing for it but to reveal our true identities, give away as little information as possible and rely on the French police ultimately releasing us. "You are right," I said. "I am a British officer and I have come here to find Frenchmen who will join the Allied cause for the day when France will be liberated from the Germans. As you can see I have only been here a very short time." They appeared to think this over.

"There are no Germans here," one of the policemen said, sounding, nevertheless, rather more friendly than before. "You are under arrest for entering France illegally."

They went on questioning me for a couple of hours. I maintained firmly that I had been dropped alone. It was clear that they knew nothing of the whereabouts, or even the existence, of my two companions. I was relieved to find that they had no knowledge of the Nérauds or the house in the Rue Blatin. The only point on which I was vulnerable and on which they interrogated me over and over again was how I might be intending to communicate with my headquarters. Towards evening, to provide a distraction and to ease the pressure I was beginning to feel, I said, "I'm afraid

I can't answer any more questions. This is the end of my working hours!" The effect was electric. The senior officer seized my chin and shook me violently, muttering at the same time something about my intolerable insolence. However, I was pleased to see that he had been distracted from the theme of his questioning. There ensued a period of relaxation. I asked the police officers, jokingly, whether maybe they might like to join the Free French organization themselves. They declined with some amusement and ended the interrogation. I overheard one say to the other, "He's more sympathetic than some of the others, isn't he." What others, I wondered. Still I was glad to be considered more sympathetic. I asked to go to the loo, thinking perhaps I might be able to escape through a window. No chance — I was never out of sight of one or other of the policemen.

That evening I was put in a cell with only a barred window very high up, given a blanket and the door locked on me by a rather gruff jailer. I lay down on the sloping bare boards and had plenty of time to think about my position. My overriding feeling was a sense of humiliation at the ease with which I had been caught, the collapse of my cover story and the need to reveal my real identity. The Werthers had been compromised but all the other elements of our embryo organization were so far intact. But there was no denying it, I had personally failed in my mission, and that almost as soon as it had begun. I had sympathized with the sufferings of the French people. Now, I thought with grim irony, I was certainly in it with them. I pulled the blanket over myself and settled as best I could to a restless night, turning over every time that the boards became too painfully hard.

The following day was taken up by the various irritating formalities apparently dictated by the French judicial system. There was no more interrogation and the Inspector in charge was quite friendly. There was, however, no sign whatever that he might be prepared to let me escape. Towards evening I was transferred to the *Prison Militaire* (known locally as the PM). I was greeted (definitely not the right word!) by a singularly disagreeable warder who searched my pockets and informed me that all warders were to be called "*Chef*". He relented to the point of giving me a bowl of "*soupe*", i.e. leaves of lettuce floating in water, giving me two army blankets, a thin straw mattress and locking me in a cell. It was dark and I ate my lettuce leaves by hand. Then I lay down on the mattress — known as a *paillasse*. It was more comfortable than the police cell, or I was already becoming more inured to life as a prisoner of the Vichy régime, and slept much better than the night before. The next day I had my hair clipped and was allotted a permanent cell. The *Chefs* however, on finding out that I was a a *parachutiste anglais* became markedly more friendly.

I discovered that the Werther brothers were also in the PM but it was only possible to exchange a few words with them when we were allowed in to the more than primitive washing facilities. Once a week we were shaved by the prison barber. Our only reading material was, curiously, the memoirs of a famous cook. This did little to make up for the lack of food — our daily ration mostly consisted of the eternal watery *soupe* about 400 grms of bread and a small piece of cheese or, occasionally, an extraordinarily tough piece of meat.

The days lengthened into weeks. It is a curious fact that, in prison, the days seem interminable but the weeks pass with remarkable speed. One day I was called to the warders' office. A parcel had arrived; it was from Madame Werther. It was opened in front of me. I saw bread, cake, cheese and other goodies. The bread and cake were cut in half to see if they might contain a saw but otherwise were kept intact. I retired to my cell with simple happiness. Such was life as it had become.

The next stage of my incarceration was strictly in accordance with French law. I was accompanied on foot by two warders to the office of the *Juge d'Instruction*, Colonel Leprêtre. This gentleman was quite friendly, had my file in front of him, talked amiably enough and told me that I would be sent for trial in due course. He also informed me that, in accordance with French law, I had been allotted a lawyer to help me prepare my defence.

I recall my meeting with this representative of the legal profession on two counts. First I was eating at about 12 o'clock an absolutely delicious bowl of beans (the first and last time the prisoners of the PM had been given such a dish!) when I was informed by a warder that my *défenseur* was waiting downstairs. I was forced to gobble my beans instead of savouring every mouthful and then followed the *Chef*. The *défenseur* was a pleasant enough young man. In the course of a rather desultory discussion I thought I would suggest that he might help me escape. He shook his head and then said in words I have not forgotten, "*Montrez-vous les plus forts et tout le monde sera avec vous*." Were these not the very words of Thrasymachus in Plato's *Republic*? "Justice is the interests of the strong." Socrates, as I recalled, had virtually spent the rest of *The Republic* in endeavouring to refute Thrasymachus, but had he succeeded?

It was not to be forgotten that the PM was under the control of the vestigial army which the Germans had decided to allow the Vichy régime to keep in the *Zone Libre*. Among other things, the prisoners, and presumably the soldiers, were awakened at 6 o'clock in the morning to a bugle sounding the reveille. After a few weeks we, or at least I, had become quite accustomed to this means of introducing another dreary day. I had heard, via a whispered communication from one of the more friendly warders, of the Allied landings in North Africa. Although this was exciting news it seemed unlikely to have any effect on my situation.

One day, about the middle of November 1942, there was no sound of the bugle and the warder appeared delayed in making his usual call. At last he appeared in a state markedly different from his usual early-morning grumpiness. During the night, he said, German troops had entered the *Zone Libre* and a sizeable detachment with tanks had surrounded the Vichy army in Clermont Ferrand, disbanded it and now occupied its barracks. The PM was totally under the control of the Germans!

The day passed uneventfully enough. The prisoners were given their rations of bread and the usual watery vegetables. Toward the evening I was summoned to the Chief Warder's office. There Colonel Leprêtre was waiting for me. He abruptly informed me, perhaps slightly apologetically, that he saw no alternative but to hand me over to the Germans. I cannot pretend that this was not a very unpleasant shock. The Germans would obviously mean the Gestapo. A vista of interrogation under torture was opening before my eyes. I felt it was incumbent on me to keep my dismay to myself. I remarked, as stiffly as I could, that if the Colonel considered that this was his only course I would just have to accept it. The warder then led me back to my cell. I meditated for a while on the very disagreeable prospect which lay before me. Finally I ate a large piece of cake which was part of one of the fortnightly parcels which Madame Werther had sent me. Then I lay down on my *paillasse*, pulled the blanket to my ears and fell into a peaceful sleep! (I should say that I have been blessed with an ability to fall asleep under nearly all circumstances and at any time!) I was awakened around midnight (my watch had been taken from me when I entered the PM) by a warder and another prisoner who I knew had been arrested for some kind of anti-Vichy activity. They told me in whispers that they would never let me be handed over to the Germans. They did not say exactly how this was to be avoided. However, thus reassured, I immediately went to sleep again!

The next day or two passed in an uneasy calm. From my cell window I could see the occasional man in civilian clothes — whether German or French I was unable to make out. Finally one of the warders gave the order that I was to be moved out of the PM within the hour. I ate two potatoes and a piece of cheese from my parcel to provide some stamina for a possible escape! As it turned out there was no such chance. The Werthers, three other prisoners and I were taken, heavily guarded by warders, from the PM to a train destined for Riom, about 20kms north of Clermont Ferrand. From the station we were marched to the local prison (the *Maison d'Arrêt*). In spite of our relief at being clear of the Germans, it had to be admitted that our first night in the *Maison d'Arrêt* was singularly unpleasant! The Werthers, three other anti-Vichy men and I were placed in a hall which already contained about twenty men all of whom turned out to be the local population of burglars and other assorted criminals! However, the following morning the six of us were separated from the rest and installed in a large room by ourselves. This, and an annexe, would be our quarters for the next two and a half months. We were allowed to receive parcels and, though the rations were meagre, the warders were entirely friendly — not friendly enough, however, to allow us to escape. It was certainly a considerable change for me — from solitary confinement to the constant companionship of five friends. Christmas and the New Year came and went. Madame Werther continued to send us parcels as did the friends and relatives of the other members of our group. Heaven knows how they managed it. Food was an obsession. It so happened that one of our companions, named Rébert, had been the proprietor of a biscuit factory in Alsace. He spent a whole day carefully drawing all the different kinds of biscuits which had been his factory's output in pre-war days! There was a small iron stove in the middle of our "living-room". Every day a warder brought us enough wood to heat it for about an hour. We gathered round it in the afternoon, keeping such rations as we had for the occasion. We called ourselves "*les Mammouths*", presumably in anticipation of our post-war appetites!

I learned much later that Brian and George had remained undisturbed by the Vichy police. They had established radio contact with F Section and had succeeded in putting together a sizeable organization of *résistants*. They had planned to mount an operation to rescue us from the *Maison d'Arrét* at Riom but were forestalled. In fact, about the middle of January 1943 orders had come through to the *Gardien Chef* of the *Maison d'Arrét* that we were to be transferred to the Prison St Paul at Lyon.

The journey to Lyon was without incident. We were then handcuffed and led through the streets of Lyon to the wrong prison! The mistake was soon remedied and we, Roger and Maurice Werther and I were duly delivered to the *Maison d'Arrét de St Paul*. Here we were separated and I was put into a cell by myself. The warders were relatively respectful. There were more than a few *résistants* among the prisoners, including one who appeared to be in total control of the prison!

He arranged for me to have a special sign on my bowl so that the warder on duty would allow me more food. The cell I was in had previously been occupied by an RAF officer (how he had got there I had no idea) who had left the emblem of the Air Force drawn on the wall. In a little time, the emblem of the Royal Fusiliers was standing beside it!

From St Paul there seemed no hope of escape.

The intention of the Vichy government was still, as it clearly had been all along, to bring me, together with the Werther brothers, to a formal trial. In retrospect I can now see that someone (I have no idea who it might have been) had decided that to avoid my falling into the hands of the Gestapo, I should be made to comply with all the rigours of the French Law. This would be a demonstration of the anti-allied policy of the Vichy Government.

I was given another lawyer, replacing my *défenseur* from Clermont Ferrand and the trial was fixed for 14 February 1943. On that day I was escorted to a police van divided into compartments to be driven to the courthouse. I was locked into one of the compartments with a respectable-looking middle-aged gentleman. He politely inquired what I might be being tried for. Replying that I was a *parachutiste anglais*, I asked what he might be accused of. He replied "Rape"! Before we could converse further we were already being off-loaded at the courthouse of the City of Lyon.

The chamber in which Roger and Maurice Werther and I were to be tried was impressively old-fashioned. We were arrayed in the dock, our defence counsels in front of us. At one side sat a number of warders. Alongside them were some men in civilian clothes possibly, even probably, members of the Gestapo. They were presumably there to oversee how the Vichy authorities would deal with "subversive elements" in what was now evidently a show trial.

The judges, three of them, dressed in stately robes, took their seats and the trial began. The state prosecutor accused me at some length of having "*survolé le territoire Français dans un aeronef étranger*," literally of having overflown French territory in a foreign flying machine. There seemed to be no mention of any subversive activities, either against Vichy or the German occupation. Roger and Maurice Werther were accused of hiding me. My *défenseur*, who appeared more concerned than had been his colleague in Clermont-Ferrand, pleaded that *survoler* really amounted to nothing more than a *contravention*, similar to an infringement of traffic regulations. At the end of the proceedings, I made a short speech stating that my only objective had been the furtherance of the French cause. More speeches ensued and then the judges retired to consider the case. It was not long before they returned. The senior judge (the President) then announced the verdicts. Roger Werther and I were each condemned to five years of *travaux forçés* (hard labour), Maurice Werther was to go free.

Roger and I were escorted to the cells beside the courtroom. There were some Jewish prisoners there awaiting transport to Germany, ostensibly to work in industry. They had managed to smuggle in some wine and were kind enough to pass a glass each to Roger and me. It was Châteauneuf du Pape and we found it very cheering. We did not know, of course, to what a terrible fate those friendly Jews were almost certainly destined. Shortly afterwards we were returned to our cells in St Paul. A notice was put on my door. "Very dangerous prisoner. To be watched every half-hour". I thought this was rather a compliment! A few days went by, mainly memorable for an unpleasant attack of indigestion, perhaps due to the diet of bread and potatoes with which I was particularly favoured. One afternoon I had my hair clipped; it had grown quite a bit since the days of the PM. I was then permitted to take a shower and returned to my cell for the night. In the afternoon of the following day, about 20 February, I joined up with Roger and five other *résistants*. These included a warder who had tried to help the other prisoners to escape. The operation had failed and he was now a prisoner himself.

We were handcuffed together and, in prison uniform, led through the streets of Lyon to the station. The warders were not unfriendly but showed no inclination to let anyone escape!

It appeared that our destination was to be Villeneuve-sur-Lot and a prison named the *Maison Centrale d'Eysses* at which we were to serve our sentences. I had visions of digging ditches, returning to a healthy meal of bread and soup and, while outside, getting the chance to slip away unnoticed. The reality was to be very different. Our journey was relatively comfortable. One of the warders gave me a sizeable chunk of bread and I slept most of the way. We had our own compartment. At one station, about midnight, a young man looking for a seat looked into our compartment, then shouted to his friend, "*Ce sont des forçats* (convicts)"! The train passed through Monluçon (I remembered going on holiday when the train from Paris to the Auvergne passed through it) and then to Limoges. We finally ended up early in the morning in Périgueux (once famous for its pâté de foie gras!) There the St Paul warders handed us over to a new set of uniformed men. It is a fact that when one is a prisoner and by definition helpless, any change, however small, in accommodation or in personnel results in a reaction of unease — the known is replaced by the menacing unknown.

We were transported in two open trucks from Périgueux to the town of Villeneuve-sur-Lot, in the environs of which the *Maison Centrale* was situated.

What must have been the usual procedure with incoming prisoners was applied to our little group. Our meagre belongings and civilian clothes were placed in a bag and ticketed. We were then issued with a different prison uniform, taken to the showers and then marched into what turned out to be the *quartier disciplinaire*. A warder asked me what crime I had been guilty of. On my replying that I was a *parachutiste anglaise* he became somewhat less gruff. I was allotted Cell No. 101.

The régime at the *Maison Centrale* was simple, monotonous and, in March 1943, had to be strictly complied with. Whenever the door of the cell opened the prisoner was required to rush to the back of the cell and stand to attention. In the morning blankets were rolled up and put outside by a "trusty"; at the same time the prisoner's trousers, which had been taken from him for the night, were returned. A bowl of watery vegetables followed with the daily bread ration of 350–400grms. More so-called *soupe* came the prisoner's way at midday and a further, rather more substantial ration together with a chunk of meat or cheese consisted the evening meal. The meat was exceptionally tough and mostly quite uneatable. The cheese usually comprised a small piece of Roquefort. Sometimes quite good and eagerly consumed, sometimes populated by large numbers of "jumping maggots". These curious creatures, the likes of which I have not seen before or since would take off from a piece of Roquefort and land on the table at a range of, say, 10 cms. In half an hour the table was covered in a circle centred on the piece of Roquefort!

Blankets were allowed in and trousers removed at around 6.30. Twice at night the light was switched on and the warder on duty checked that each prisoner was present.

The monotony was mildly relieved by the *travaux forçes*. This was far from the ditch digging operations of my imaginings. It consisted of what can best be described as "cows' veils". In the south of France cows are, or were, used to pull carts or farm implements. To shield their faces from the flies which abound there in the summer, the farmers bind a rectangle of mesh made from string to the cow's forehead covering its eyes. The manufacture of these was the *travaux forçes*. The more adept prisoners were able to produce one veil a day.

The "trusty" who supervised the operation was a cheerful fellow who was in prison for having forged 18,000 bread coupons. Apparently an expert in the matter of "cows' veils", he unkindly characterised my efforts as "*parmi les mauvés ils sont mediocres*"! All the same, at the end of a month or so I was able to produce one a day — of a sort!

Solitary confinement is, by definition, an excellent opportunity for reflection. The warders became relatively friendly. Mme Werther sent me periodical parcels, without which I would probably have starved, and occasional French school classics. I wrote a small number of essays on philosophy and psychology, subjects in which I had always been interested. One might think that solitary confinement was an ideal situation in which to explore the experiences of philosophical or religious contemplation. Although sometimes, in the evening, after the warders had gone their rounds and locked us up for the night, I did manage to achieve a kind of mental or spiritual detachment, the overriding urge to escape made this difficult. Also the lack of food. Although we hear of monks and hermits leading lives of extreme asceticism I have to admit that I was not one of them!

In the course of my imprisonment I learnt that it is much easier to endure hunger during the day than at night. I used to store up such food as I had to eat at night. I discovered that in this way I was able to keep warmer and sleep better. Sex? What about a plate of ham and eggs? Such was my life until sometime after Easter, celebrated by a bowlful of rice — a celebration indeed!

There was a slow but noticeable change in the attitude of the warders. They occasionally whispered items of war news. I recall one morning when I was putting out my blankets the warder on duty whispered, "*Mille bombardiers sur Essen*." Towards the end of April the Deputy Governor of the *Maison Centrale* on his fortnightly inspection murmured, "*Il fait chaud en Afrique*." The tide was evidently turning against the Axis. Then the supply of string for the "cows' veils" ran out. There was really nothing to do except sleep. Even I had enough of it.

One day someone, I have no idea who it might have been, sent me a book. It was in English and was a comprehensive American social study entitled *Middletown Revisited*. This book was something of a revelation. It consisted of a systematic survey of attitudes, tastes and habits in an American community and introduced me to a new way of viewing human society. I finished it towards the end of May 1943.

Finally I decided to approach the most friendly warder. I slipped a note into his hand offering Frs. 100,000 if he would let me escape. I would pay him when I got out. When he came round again he shook his head. However, he did not report me to his supervisor.

CHAPTER THREE

Out of France

Life changed completely for the prisoners of the *Maison Centrale* about the middle of June 1943. Probably it coincided with the Vichy authorities, or at least some of them, realizing that the Allies would eventually win the war. Whatever the cause, the discipline of the prison became greatly relaxed. No more standing to attention at the back of one's cell whenever the door was opened. Roger Werther was moved into my cell and on that day we had a good deal to talk about! Shortly afterwards we were allowed out of our cells during daytime and our civilian clothes were given back to us, replacing the uniforms. It turned out that the *Maison Centrale*'s population was being rapidly transformed from individuals sentenced for criminal activities to those who were detained for resistance to the Germans or to Vichy. It should be explained that under the French system of *travaux forçes* prisoners serving five-year sentences had to serve one year in solitary confinement (those with longer sentences served two or three years). Thus it was that Roger and I and numerous other members of resistance organisations had been consigned to cells in the so-called *quartier disciplinaire* — in all about sixty men. In the main part of the prison, sleeping in dormitories, was a very much larger group, maybe a thousand strong. We were now able to contact these and among them I found a few men associated with SOE. One of them was Philippe de Vômecourt. Another was Jean Aron who was moved into Cell No. 101.

Needless to say, in this new much more favourable situation we began seriously concocting plans to escape. The entire prison was surrounded by a five-metre wall with watchtowers every hundred metres or so. These watchtowers were manned by local guards, who had in earlier months disturbed our sleep by shouting every hour during the night "*Prenez garde à vous*". Contact with some of these showed that they were quite friendly and would probably not interfere with any attempt to escape. Another member of our group was André Léscorat and was to become a most valuable asset. Léscorat had been mayor of his village before his arrest and possessed contacts throughout the whole area of Department of the Lot.

In the autumn of 1943, while we were engaged in discussing various plans for escape, I happened to get a nasty cold. This developed into an attack of bronchial asthma so bad that I could hardly breathe. What chance I had of escaping looked rather bleak. The prison doctor gave me some medicine which proved quite useless. Eventually I struggled to the infirmary where a medical student kindly gave me an enormous shot of adrenaline. Shaking like a jelly I sat under a tree in the yard of the infirmary — momentarily cured of asthma. From then on I gradually improved.

We had our plans ready by early December for an escape which would involve all the resistance men in the *Quartier Disciplinaire* and some others of whom we had our doubts as to their abilities, or to their genuineness, or both. We were, however, presented with the necessity of making a very serious decision. We knew that the prisoners in the main part of the prison had for some time been preparing for a general breakout of all the prisoners. Even arms had been smuggled in. We could be certain that if our attempt succeeded, and even if it did not, discipline would be sharply tightened in the *Maison Centrale* and the warders and the guards in the watch-towers would be changed — perhaps to be replaced by the detested Vichy *Milice* or even German troops. As December passed nothing positive was emerging from the leaders of the men in the main prison. Circumstances would never be more favourable. We decided to take our chance on the evening of the third of January 1944.

It is a fact that in the world of plots and underground activities no matter how plotters and planners enjoin secrecy upon their fellow conspirators, somehow what they are plotting and planning will leak out, and sooner rather than later. There is only one remedy for this. Spread as many stories — all ultra-confidential of course — as possible, thus totally confusing the issue! In our case we gave out a variety of dates on which we might try our escape. We were pleased to see that no-one took us seriously!

We knew by this time that most of the warders of the *Quartier Disciplinaire* would either shut their eyes or actively participate in our escape. However, there was a group led by Philippe de Vômecourt comprising half-a-dozen men in the main part of the prison whom we had specially picked, either because of their connection with the Firm or for their particular skills, e.g. a radio operator named, or code-named, Tanon. These would have to be led to the Q.D. just in time for the operation.

We knew that we would have to be in some kind of hideout before dawn. The Vichy authorities would be sure to make an extensive search of the area as soon as it was daylight. Léscorat recommended that we should head for the area around Cancon. He had contacts with the farmers there and was able to transmit a message, through his visitors, that they might expect to receive some fugitives at an undefined date! Cancon was about 20 kms by road from Villeneuve-sur-Lot, but would be good deal longer walking cross-country, as we would be obliged to do.

On 3 January at 17.30 hours, just as the light was beginning to fade but before all the prisoners were locked in for the night, I went round all the cells. It was felt that my status as an allied agent would give my injunctions most weight. All the more that I had promoted myself "commandant" for the occasion! I said to the inmates of each cell, "In a quarter of an hour the prison doors will be opened. If you want to escape be ready and follow the lead which we will give you." I then returned to the ground floor entrance.

Here my companions were making ready. We took with us such items of warm clothing as we possessed and not much else. The men of the various resistance organizations, twenty in all, were divided into three groups of six or seven each; to these would be added, in the prison yard of the *Quartier Discipline*, six of the group from the main prison led by de Vômecourt and a helpful warder. This comprised a total of twenty-six, all of whom were judged to be useful in terms their potential contribution to the resistance organizations.

Another couple of dozen men would be allowed to escape with us. These would have to fend for themselves. They were certainly a motley lot: Spanish Communists who had fled into France when Franco had triumphed in the Civil War, a man who gave himself out to be a Colonel in the French Army but who was thought to be an NCO who had been convicted of rape, and a brilliant and extremely woolly mathematician. This crowd assembled behind our three groups in the main hall of the Q.D. One warder, named Yvan Gaillard, had decided to throw in his lot with us. Another, though sympathetic, declined our invitation. Thinking, with some justification, that the prison authorities would be sure to accuse him of complicity in our escape, he acted a role in which, by endeavouring to prevent us getting out, he had been beaten up. To this end he threw himself about, falling on the corner of a table and, as we heard later, breaking ribs. We locked him in one of the cells and took his keys. (In fact the damage to his ribs was a decisive factor subsequently in acquitting him of the accusation of complicity.)

At precisely 17.45 the de Vômecourt group, accompanied by Gaillard, entered the courtyard of the Q.D. Simultaneously we threw open the doors and I ordered each group with minimal interval to proceed into the walkway between the prison buildings and the perimeter wall. The leading group consisted of particularly tough customers in the event of anyone trying to check us at this stage. My own group went last and then the crowd of miscellaneous characters followed. I put on the cap of the warder who had remained locked up!

About 100 metres from the Q.D. was a gate through the perimeter wall. Gaillard opened it; one warder who attempted to hold us up was easily dealt with by the "tough customers" and to our relief the armed guards on the watchtowers did not interfere. When I passed through, leading the last group, the sense of freedom, after the long months of waiting, was overwhelming. As soon as we were out of sight of the watchtowers I threw the warder's cap into a ditch.

According to plan all four groups would proceed to a rendezvous in the neighbourhood of Cancon. On the way we kept well separated so as to attract less notice.

Some members of what I have termed "the motley crowd" decided that they would like to join onto the last group — mine. One of my companions, Blondet by name, asked me to "hand him the pistol"; in fact we were quite unarmed. However, they quickly elected to go elsewhere!

The night trek by the four groups was more than a little strenuous. Months in captivity had made our muscles soft, not to speak of the diet, or absence of it. In my own case, my legs had swelled considerably. However, the fact that we were free made us forget everything else. We had some difficulty in finding a way which would avoid as many main roads and villages as possible, with only a Michelin map to guide us. I particularly distinguished myself by leading my group in a complete circle! My friends quietly deposed me as guide for the rest of the night! In the end we called at a farmhouse and a helpful peasant put us on our way. Once we were about 5 kms clear of Villeneuve-sur-Lot we decided to walk along the road leading towards Cancon. We kept in single file keeping to the edge and avoiding any traffic by diving into the bushes whenever we saw the lights of a car. There was, of course, a curfew and we only saw a car once. It turned out to be the prison van obviously looking for escaped prisoners!

There were villages on the route which we considered we must avoid by making a detour. This greatly delayed our progress. The countryside of the Department of the Lot is covered with vineyards and the wires which support the vines were still in place although it was winter. This made for endless clambering over them which in the near-darkness and the muddy ground was particularly time-consuming and physically demanding.

Although we made the detours round the villages quite wide, this was not enough to escape the attention of the local dogs. Fortunately they were chained up, though their furious barking must have awakened the neighbourhood. However, their owners either slept remarkably well or did not venture out of doors. We were even able to trace the progress of at least one of our groups by the distant dogs' chorus!

As dawn was beginning to break we reached our rendezvous point. According to the map this was a bridge over a railway about 3 kms north of Cancon. It turned out that the railway no longer existed — the tracks had been torn up. The bridge, however, was still there, but Léscorat's contacts were nowhere to be seen. There was almost full daylight by this time and in desperation I knocked on the door of a nearby farm. A woman's voice answered but when I hastily explained our need and appealed to her patriotism total silence ensued. We went back to the bridge and to our great relief a member of one of our groups, named Raimond Glaesner, a sturdy and courageous Alsatian, met us. We followed him at top speed and he led us a short distance to one of the farms which had been part of Léscorat's organization before his arrest. Here we joined up with all four of the groups which had set out from the *Maison Centrale* the night before. The farmer had indeed been warned to expect some escapees. The only problem was that he had been expecting maybe three or four men. He was surprised that we numbered twenty-six! It was in fact remarkable that all those (around fifty-five) who escaped from the Q.D. of the *Maison Centrale* that night were hidden among the population of the Lot by the following day. Truly marvellous in view of the risk of deportation or imprisonment which were run by all who concealed "subversive elements", as they were called.

All twenty-six of us were accommodated for the day in the loft of a barn. We were given bottles of wine and water to drink — badly needed as our exertions had left us extremely dehydrated — and bread and cheese. Some time during the morning we were urgently commanded to be totally silent. Apparently the gendarmes were going from farm to farm searching for any trace of the men who had escaped from the *Maison Centrale*. Our farmer and his family evidently managed to reassure the gendarmes as to his complete ignorance of what they were talking about and they passed on to question his neighbours. We heard later that they had questioned the woman on whose door I had knocked and who had refused to have anything to do with us. Her information gave the impression that we had been making our way north of Cancon whereas in fact we had gone about a kilometre south of the house where I had been given such a cold reception. This, very usefully, put the gendarmes on a false scent!

During the next days the ex-prisoners were spread out into the countryside in the general area of Cancon. This was entirely the doing of the resistance *réseau* of which Léscorat had been the leader before his arrest. De Vômecourt and I had already selected the men whom we considered particularly reliable and were otherwise unattached to any one of the major French resistance organizations for recruitment into the "Firm". The remainder, by their own choice, rejoined the organizations to which they had originally belonged, notably "Combat", "Liberation" and "Francs-Tireurs".

It was at this point that "Hilaire" — Major (later Lt. Col.) George Starr — was able to report to Maurice Buckmaster that de Vômecourt and I had successfully escaped from the *Maison Centrale*. We were ordered to return to the U.K. together with the fourteen men we had selected. About mid-January we moved from our safe house in the Cancon area. Apparently in the Lot region Cancon was known by the phrase "*Cancon, petite ville mauvais renom. Une putain dans chaque maison"!* (Little town, bad reputation. A whore in every house.) Whatever its reputation the people of Cancon risked their lives by hiding us in their homes.

For several days Philippe de Vômecourt and I were hidden on the farm of M and Mme Vielcazat three or four kilometres southwest of Cancon. I well remember the kindness with which they treated us as we were recovering from the effects of our escape.

During the next four weeks I saw very little of my ex-companions of the *Maison Centrale*. There was one rather hair-raising experience, however. The sixteen of us, destined, we hoped, for SOE, were to be moved from the Cancon area to the neighbourhood of Agen. For this manoeuvre Hilaire's *réseau* had somehow commandeered a large prison van (the French equivalent of a Black Maria) complete with two uniformed gendarmes. This vehicles went the round of the safe houses where we were hidden, picking up our group of sixteen. We were then locked in and the "Black

Maria" proceeded along the main road towards Agen, with the gendarmes obviously on guard!

All went smoothly enough until, about ten kilometres from Agen, the "Black Maria" broke down. What was the matter with it we had no idea. The gendarmes unlocked the doors and if anyone had been watching he would have been treated to the spectacle of sixteen prisoners pushing the "Black Maria" for two or three hundred metres. At this point the engine came to life, the prisoners were duly locked in again and no further hitches occurred until we were distributed amongst safe houses belonging to the Hilaire *réseau*. If any of the staff of the *Maison Centrale* had happened to pass us just as we were pushing the "Black Maria" the situation might have been quite uncomfortable!

I spent the next few days in the flat of a police inspector, again a member of the Hilaire *réseau*, who then took me to a house in Albi. This belonged to a local industrialist whose wife was British. I was made a temporary member of the family — there were two daughters and three or four dogs — and fed enormous quantities of *pommes frites* and generally recuperated after the various episodes of the preceding weeks.

After some ten days the same inspector came to transfer me to yet another safe house. This time it was to be the residence of a family of vinegrowers in the Armagnac — famous for its brandy. Here once more I was made to feel at home. Hilaire (George Starr), together with his assistant Anne-Marie Walters who had been dropped by parachute some months previously, informed me that our entire group was scheduled to cross the Pyrenees in about two weeks' time. In the meantime I was to be patient! From my mountaineering days in the Alps I realized that any crossing of the Pyrenees in winter would certainly be a strenuous undertaking, nor would the need to avoid the German troops guarding the French-Spanish border be likely to make it any easier! I spent my days walking up and down a track through the vineyards. Not much in the way of training after fifteen months of incarceration, but better than nothing.

In the family the Armagnac flowed like water. They even used it to clean the windows! The son of the house took me down to the cellars. Here the noble liquid was stored to mature in huge barrels. He pointed to a particularly large one. This, he said, was awaiting the Allied soldiers to celebrate the liberation of France! I declared myself a teetotaller and got away without having to do more than occasionally to drink the health of my friends.

At length a car with Anne-Marie came to collect me and, after a shortish drive, we came to a barn-like building near Auch where all the sixteen members, ex-*Maison Centrale*, were reunited. We were kitted out with boots and clothes for the Pyrenean expedition. How the members of the Hilaire *réseau* were able to obtain such an amount of equipment in the circumstances prevailing in France in 1944, I shall never know.

That afternoon we again boarded the "Black Maria" and proceeded without incident to Arreau. Here we were deposited in a café — the proprietor was, needless to say, a member of the Hilaire *réseau*. There followed a very uncomfortable quarter of an hour. Arreau was in the *zone interdite*, which was under close German control. Sixteen men, aged 22 to 38, would be extremely conspicuous to anyone passing the café and would be certain to attract the attention of any member of the German frontier forces. The little town seemed to be almost deserted.

At length a large truck arrived and we hurried to board it. It turned out that this truck was used to carry the rations for the men working on a dam which was part of a hydro-electric scheme at Tramezaygues. Although the whole project had been suspended for the duration of the war there was still a crew of maintenance men. Their accommodation and *cantine* were under the supervision of the driver of the truck and his wife Danielle. The truck regularly carried the rations for the *cantine* and the German frontier guards were quite used to it. Sure enough we stopped at a kind of depot. The sixteen of us were instructed to squeeze ourselves as tightly as possible into the freight-carrying part of the truck and on no account to talk or make any noise.

The remainder of the truck was piled to the roof with cabbages, sacks of flour and potatoes, and we set off. After about twenty minutes we were stopped at what must have been a German guard post. We heard a few words of conversation, someone seemed to look into the back of the truck. With what seemed to be cheerful salutation, to our considerable relief, the truck started and we were on our way.

It took us another half-hour, climbing steadily, to reach the huts of the barrage works. There were quite a few of them, now mostly empty. We were put quickly into two rooms next to the supervisor's quarters — eight to each. We were given a bowl of potatoes and cabbage and Philippe de Vômecourt and I talked during the evening to our hosts. They were a most courageous and resourceful couple and had contacts on the Spanish side of the Pyrenees. They seemed oblivious to the risks they were taking.

The following day the *passeur*, as the Pyrenean guides were known, came to see us. He was a rather fine-looking man, a Spaniard who could not speak French. His name was Angel and we would be completely in his hands for the crossing. Curiously enough it did not occur to me that he might simply sell us to the Germans.

The next day there was a snowstorm and Angel said the crossing was quite impossible. The following day was equally bad. Another source of worry was one of our group, Stargart by name. We had taken him because he had declared himself to be a Czech pilot of the RAF who had been shot down in a Beaufighter. We could not know whether his story was true or not but he seemed a sturdy character and had been for some time in the *Maison Centrale*. Now he had somehow caught a cold which had developed into a nasty chest infection, accompanied by continuous coughing and wheezing. He was manifestly unfit for the kind of journey which lay ahead of us. Very reluctantly he let himself be persuaded to stay on in the *cantine*. Angel agreed to guide him over the mountains as soon as he might be fit again.

Our unscheduled protracted stay in the *cantine* was an increasing cause for anxiety. A French gendarme called in on Danielle and her husband and was duly entertained to ersatz coffee whilst we hid in a nearby room. The gendarme went on his way apparently suspecting nothing, but every day increased the danger. There were one or two last-minute thoughts which stood us in good stead. From my mountaineering experience in Switzerland I felt that some twenty metres of solid rope might come in handy. Philippe thought that some good sticks could be useful to those less sure of their footholds.

At last the clouds cleared; it was the evening of our fourth day in the *cantine*. We did our best to show our gratitude to Danielle and her husband. She used to sing a song while working in her flat, next to the two rooms which were our hiding place. The refrain went like this: "*Un chemin va qui va qui va — et qui ne revient pas*." It seemed rather appropriate. I have not forgotten it.

It was the morning of 17 February 1944, almost exactly a year since I had appeared before the "Tribunal" in Lyon. At 4a.m. we ate a piece of bread with the usual cup of ersatz coffee and moved out of the *cantine* in single file with Angel in the lead. The snow was surprisingly deep. Although we endeavoured as far as possible to keep in each other's footsteps we nevertheless produced a track which would surely be evident to the German frontier guards. After a short stretch of flat ground we began to climb quite steeply.

The day was beginning to break now. I could only hope that, if our tracks were discovered, the Germans, not knowing when we had made them, would not think it worthwhile pursuing us into the mountains.

After about three hours we took a short break. We were already above the tree line and the peaks of the central Pyrenees stood high above us. I felt a sense of exhilaration — after all I had been brought up in the mountains and it began to look as though the chance of the Germans following our tracks was beginning to recede. This feeling was short-lived; the angle of the slope up which Angel was guiding us steepened sharply and with increasing altitude the fresh snow lay ever deeper. Suddenly Tanon declared that he could go no further and that we must abandon him. This was not to be thought of; he would either be captured by the Germans or be benighted and probably die of exposure. I tied the rope we had brought with us, putting Tanon in the middle, myself at one end and Raimond Glaesner at the other. The two of us then pulled Tanon up the interminable snow slopes. Some of our younger companions relieved us from time to time. To my own surprise I turned out to be about the fittest of the group. Eventually the angle began to ease off and the wind had swept the new snow from the highest ridges. Tanon was able to get along unaided.

For a few minutes I experienced an unpleasant feeling of weakness, probably a reaction from the effort of pulling and towing. Philippe, always resourceful, pulled two lumps of sugar from his pocket and gave them to me. Eating them, I felt the strength flowing back into my legs. The col (it was called the Riou-majou) was now in sight. Half an hour afterwards we stood on the top looking downward into Spain. It was probably about three of four in the afternoon.

Another short break, a piece of bread, and we were on our way again, downhill this time and, curiously, with much less snow than on the French side. Eventually we came to a path which led us to a small village at about eight o'clock in the evening. We were made marvellously welcome by the inhabitants who must have been connected in some way to Angel. We had seen nothing of the Spanish border guards. We had heard that if they happened to catch anyone escaping over the Pyrenees in the immediate vicinity of the frontier they would be escorted back, almost certainly into the hands of the Germans. Those who were caught further away from the frontier could expect to be interned for, maybe, two or three months until they were ransomed by the British Embassy for, it was said, a cubic metre of petrol!

Meanwhile we relaxed with food, wine and an absolutely delicious Spanish liqueur! We went happily to sleep on some straw with our blankets over us — all of our struggles were over, weren't they? No, they were not! We were woken at four in the morning, hurriedly given something to eat and, again in darkness, started out of the village, across a small valley and began to climb again. The wine and liqueur had certainly not prepared us for this renewal of effort. Already our little group was beginning to straggle badly. Action was required! I placed myself immediately behind Angel and, through one of the Spanish speakers, indicated that he must walk more slowly! We walked steadily with few breaks to eat the rations our hosts of the night before had provided us with. It was towards the end of the afternoon and most of us were probably near to exhaustion when Angel went off the path and, circumventing a number of rocks and bushes, led us in about twenty minutes to two caves. This was to be our hide-out. Angel said he would bring food from the neighbouring village which was named Seira. He explained that we would be quite safe in the caves but that the police were sometimes around in the village and this could be dangerous. He reappeared in an hour or two, with a man whom he said was a cousin. Both were laden with eatables. We fell on them and then endeavoured to sleep. Endeavoured was the word, the floors of the caves were rocky and the weather was very cold. By making fires we managed to keep warm but the smoke, from branches of trees, was absolutely choking. When the fires went out we were frozen. In spite of this we were buoyed by the thought that we were progressing. The Germans had been left far behind.

The next thing was to organize some means of getting to Barcelona. In my original briefing (how far away it now seemed) I had been informed of the address of the British Consulate and provided with an identification code phrase. It was "Clan McArthur"! The following morning, after the night in the caves, I suggested to Angel that I would be ready to pay rather handsomely for a car and driver. I still had money, provided by Hilaire for such an eventuality. We settled on 30,000 French francs.

I had spent two nights in the caves and the third night we set off. I took Roger Werther and one of our number who had had his feet rather badly frostibitten on the Riou-majou. I should explain that Roger had been a member of the International Brigade on the Republican side of the Spanish Civil War, a fact which it was imperative to conceal, since all those who had been in the Brigade were liable to a long term of imprisonment by the Franco régime. However, participating in the Civil War had given him a knowledge of the Spanish language. I thought this might prove useful. How useful we were soon to see. At first our journey from Seira to Barcelona went perfectly. We passed through Barbastro and then on to Lerida. It was quite dark. In Lerida a policeman stepped from the pavement and signalled us to stop. I will admit to a feeling of utter depression. After all our struggles were we now to be placed in some kind of Spanish prison camp?

Roger was now talking volubly to the policeman. The latter seemed to ask a few questions to which Roger replied. Then to my amazement the policeman seemed almost to smile and then with a gesture of his hand indicated that we might proceed! We were on our way out of Lerida. As we left the town I said to Roger, “What on earth did you say to that policeman?” “I told him,” Roger said, “that we were RAF pilots. I even mentioned that one of us was hurt.” This was the man who had suffered from frost-bite and whose foot was in bandages. "He must have been pro-Allied. Anyway blessings on him."

Nothing further happened until we reached Barcelona. I had the address — memorized of course — of the Consulate General. I told our driver to stop a little way down the road and then, as I had been briefed, walked boldly past the Spanish policeman on duty at the door. The receptionist quickly realised that there was something unusual about me — I was filthy and unshaven but had not forgotten my English and was at once shown into the office of one of the Vice-Consuls. (I later found out that his specific task was to deal with Allied personnel who had succeeded in getting in to Spain through Occupied France.) I explained that my companions were waiting in a car only a short distance away and that they might be picked up any minute. He quickly rose to the occasion and in a very short time my two disreputable-looking companions joined me. The driver, as had been agreed, drove away as rapidly as possible. I produced my code phrase and briefly told the Vice-Consul the story of our escape. I also informed him of the plight of the remaining thirteen members of our group. He reacted by telling me to get showered, shaved and into some warm clothes — apparently the Consulate had some available for any escapees who might be in need of them. I then had something to eat and in the afternoon two cars drew up in front of the Consulate. The Vice-Consul, whose name I have forgotten, drove one of them while I put myself beside him. The other car followed. It gave me a considerable feeling of satisfaction to see the Union Jack fluttering on the bonnets of the cars!

We followed the route along which I had come with my companions the night before, via Lerida — no police check this time! At Barbastro the V-C thought that it would be getting too dark to proceed to Seira, contact Angel and his friends and then evacuate the men who would still be in the caves. A curious incident followed: the V-C could not find suitable accommodation in Barbastro. He informed me that, in the absence of identity papers, I would have to spend the night in the car anyway and we drove up to Venasque which I knew of as a ski resort, although I had never skied there. Now the whole place was deserted. We munched some delicious Consulate-prepared sandwiches in the village square and returned to Barbastro. Finally one of the hotels agreed to put the V-C into a servant's room — he accepted it with some indignation — and I wrapped myself in the back seat of the car, gloriously comfortable compared to the caves.

Early next morning we drove up the road to Seira. I was rather relieved to be able to locate the house which I had left in the dark two nights before. Angel and his friends were certainly pleased to see us. The men in the caves and the need to feed them would in time have attracted the attention of the police.

It was decided that Angel and two or three selected men would accompany the V-C to the caves and bring all the escapees down. As a non-Spanish speaker it was thought wiser for me to stay hidden in Seira. The lady of the house, thinking maybe that I looked all in, lent me a bed to sleep on. It was even better than the back of the V-C's car! I awoke to find that all of the members of our group had been fetched from the caves without a hitch. We said a more than grateful farewell to Angel, his family and friends who had helped us so splendidly, got into the cars and, with the Union Jacks proudly displayed, took the road to Barcelona. For me, at any rate, it was a true moment of elation.

CHAPTER FOUR

Interval at Home

We remained only a short time in Barcelona. We were given quarters in a house rented by the Consulate and my principal memory or our stay is the enormous quantity of beautiful oranges which we consumed. None of us had seen an orange for years and here we were able to send someone out to buy them, five kilos at a time.

It was not long before we were transferred to Madrid by car, again with the flag flying. The Embassy put us up in a small hotel, gave us false identity cards. I was a South African aged 19 (we had to be aged under 20 or over 40 to satisfy the Spanish authorities that we were not of military age) and told on no account to go out into the street. I was much tempted to defy orders and pay a visit to the Prado. Some of its marvellous pictures had been on display in Geneva while the Civil War was going on. However, I thought better of it and stayed put in the hotel. Fortunately it was not long before we were again on the move. This time we were to take the night train from Madrid to the frontier with Gibraltar. There was one sleeper and the others had to sit rather uncomfortably in second or third class carriages all night. For some reason our 19-year-old South African was adjudged the sleeper — and passed a restful night!

There was no difficulty in crossing the frontier and we were pleased to find ourselves in British army quarters. We were looked after and fed by British soldiers who, rather to my annoyance, did not seem to take us too seriously! We strolled about Gibraltar waiting impatiently for transfer to the U.K. At last the order came for Philippe de Vômecourt and me. As darkness fell over Gibraltar we climbed into an aircraft — I think it was a Dakota — and, passing well out into the Atlantic, turned into the southern U.K. We landed somewhere near Swindon. Philippe and I were separated. Then, with little formality, I was issued with a railway pass and found myself on the platform of Swindon station waiting for the train to Paddington. My orders were to report to the Railway Transport Officer at Paddington. In the train I had some time to think over what I would do on arrival. I would surely be welcomed by a member of F Section, then I would telephone my wife, who was presumably still living in Shropshire and ask her to come and meet me in London. I was also, needless to say, wanting to contact my mother and father who were probably still living in Ealing. My daughter, who I had seen the day after she was born, would now be nearly a year and a half old. What had happened to them and all my friends and relations I had, of course, no means of knowing. I was certainly looking forward to it all. I was also on a slightly euphoric wave. After all I had helped plan the escape, been a leader in the crossing of the Pyrenees and there were several potential recruits for F Section who had come with me. All in all it was with general satisfaction and a sense of anticipation that I stepped on to the platform at Paddington and walked towards the RTO.

Just as I was about to enter the office a young man in plain clothes stepped forward. He asked my name and then, in the politest and friendliest way informed me that I was under arrest! I was so shocked that I must admit to a rather hazy recollection of the events which immediately followed. It appeared that all individuals who had been in enemy hands were subject to a check-up on their activities during which time they were not allowed to communicate with anyone, their families included. The young man, who it turned out was a sergeant in the Intelligence Corps, accompanied me by taxi to Waterloo station where we got on a train for Guildford. On arrival at Guildford we again took a taxi to one of F Section's safe houses where I had been quartered for a time in the summer of 1942. The very nice English woman and her husband, who was French, must have been surprised that I was not overjoyed at seeing them again. The Intelligence sergeant asked me to write a report on what had happened to me during my time in France, adding that I would soon be contacted by my H.Q.

I settled down in a state of considerable grumpiness. I took a day or two writing the report and then told my host jailer that if something wasn't done — and quickly — I was going to escape from him, mentioning that I was in rather good practice in the art of escaping!

Whether this ultimatum did the trick I don't know. However, two days later I was summoned to a meeting with Maurice Buckmaster to whom I presented my report. He was, as always, friendly and understanding; he said that my "arrest" had been an obligatory routine and that I was now free to communicate with my family, but that I should stay in London for a few days when we could discuss my future.

I immediately telephoned my mother and father in Ealing and my wife who was at Church Stretton in Shropshire. We met at the Paddington Station hotel. They had had no news of me whatever beyond a fortnightly notification from the War Office that I was in "good health" or words to that effect. They were, I think, rather surprised at my Spanish second-hand clothes and, probably, rather scruffy appearance. It can be imagined that we talked and talked. My father, rather apologetically, said that the only hotel room he could find for us was at the Savoy. This seemed to me very suitable after the *Maison Centrale*, not to speak of the Pyrenean caves. In the extremely plush bathroom I saw a notice stating that the hotel's guests were not expected to exceed nine inches of water in their baths. I filled it to the brim! The following day — it was a Sunday — dressed in uniform, wife had brought one down from Church Stretton — we went to church in the Wren Chapel in the Strand. The bomb-damaged buildings were still much in evidence but the church seemed very peaceful. How British it all was.

In my next interview with Colonel "Buck", I asked him if I could proceed on another mission to France as rapidly as possible. I don't think he was surprised. He said I was to have a medical examination, two weeks leave, and a short course on the latest weaponry. Then I might be ready for any further plans that F Section might have set up.

I had a pleasant leave, saw my daughter who was now running about and already beginning to find a few words, and visited a number of friends and relations. It was a world in which I no longer quite fitted. I had, even in pre-war days, a certain affinity for the Stoic and Buddhist philosophers and their doctrine of detachment. This, however, was something different. True, I felt a measure of detachment from even my family and friends, but there was now a sense of belonging to a different world — the world of the underground struggle, of life-and-death loyalties and treacheries, or resistance and the Gestapo. I felt that one day, perhaps very soon, the Allies would invade France and that I must be there. It was as simple as that! My fifteen months in the *Maison Centrale* and the subsequent escape had given me a new feeling of toughness and some confidence in my ability as a leader.

It was only after the war that I learned what happened to the prisoners in the main part of the *Maison Centrale d'Eysses* after we had escaped on 3 January. As we had feared, the warders and guards were replaced either with pro-Vichy *Milice* or with soldiers of the German Army. In this situation, the prisoners, (some of them possessing the arms which had been smuggled in), finding escape impossible, seized the deputy-governor of the prison and held him hostage.

They were, however, absolutely unable to break out and reluctantly negotiated a deal in which the deputy governor would be set free. In exchange, privileges of freedom within the prison and of receiving parcels of food would be restored. In fact, once the deputy governor was freed, an iron discipline was initiated! Twelve of the ringleaders of the revolt were shot. All the others, before long, were evacuated first to a camp near Compiègne and then to concentration camps in Germany itself. Some returned to France at the end of the war, some did not. We heard that there had been great bitterness at our escape from the *Quartier Disciplinaire*. The other prisoners felt that we had selfishly spoiled their possibility of breaking out.

In retrospect, I still feel that we had to take our chance when we could. We did wait for about a month but it seemed clear at the time and even more so with hindsight that an operation involving a thousand men in German-occupied France could never have succeeded. I feel troubled, nevertheless, at the thought that we might have been coincidentally instrumental in contributing to the terrible fate which befell our fellow prisoners.

I returned to the F Section office after my course on various new weapons, most of them American. There I met up again with my old friend George Jones. George was able to recount the events which occurred after my arrest with the Werther brothers at Le Crest. For a time all had gone well. George communicated regularly with the Firm and he and Brian Rafferty had set up quite an organization. They were even planning to rescue Roger,

Maurice and me from the prison in Riom. The plan fell through, of course, when we were moved to Lyon for trial. It must have been soon after this that George fell off his bicycle, injuring himself quite seriously, and was taken to hospital in Clermont Ferrand. His identity was not discovered. However, he lost the sight of one eye but otherwise gradually recovered. He then returned to his radio set on a farm somewhere in the hills of the Auvergne.

I learned many years later that Brian Rafferty had continued actively organizing his *réseau* until June 1943. During that time he regularly reported to F Section via George Jones, except, of course, when the latter had been incapacitated by his bicycle accident. About the beginning of June 1943 Brian, with members of his *réseau* mounted an important sabotage operation on the Michelin plant at Clermont Ferrand which was at that time employed in making tyres for the German Army transport. The attack succeeded in causing a major fire in the processing units and the stores, such that all production was temporarily halted.[1]

Shortly after this remarkable success Brian was arrested by the Gestapo.

It appears that he was attempting to organize the escape of a French officer at Lons-le-Saunier. Brian had his arm broken and was severely beaten by the Gestapo, while imprisoned first in Dijon then in Fresnes. He was moved from Fresnes to Flossenberg in

---

[1] Not included in Brian's SOE file but authenticated in an Abwehr report.

April 1943 and was executed there, almost at the end of the war, on 29 March, 1945. His personnel SOE file contains the remark, "A charming officer with a great personality". I can stand as a witness to the truth of this observation.

Shortly after Brian's capture George was also arrested by the Gestapo; either they had succeeded in pinpointing his radio or someone had given him away. He was, I believe, taken to the Gestapo H.Q. at Montluçon and there subjected to numerous beatings in an attempt to get information out of him regarding the resistance network for which he operated. One day, handcuffed, he was ordered to go from the ground floor of the building to the first floor — assuredly for more questioning and beating. On the stairway he was for a moment unguarded and, passing a window which was not barred and with extreme presence of mind, he managed to leap from it to the ground. Surrounding the garden was a spiked iron fence. He raced towards it, hearing that the alarm had already been given and, handcuffed as he was, managed to clamber over it, tearing his leg on one of the spikes in the process. He ran down a piece of road outside the property and, hearing the Gestapo guards coming out of the gate in full pursuit, managed to climb over a wall in one of the neighbouring properties and lie down at the foot of it. He remained there until darkness was beginning to fall, then limped slowly down the street and took his chance by knocking on the door of a house. By sheer luck the owner and his family had a connection with the Resistance and also with a garage. Soon a sturdy character appeared with a large pair of cutters and succeeded in disposing of the handcuffs. Thereafter a doctor dressed his wound; he was fed and moved out of the town. After somehow getting in touch with the "Firm", he was ordered to return to Britain and fortunately he was able to get a lift in a Lysander aeroplane. George was certainly one of the very few people to have escaped from the prisons of the Gestapo. It should be said that an additional source of anxiety to him was the fact that he knew his father, a British subject living in Paris, had been interned by the Germans for the duration of the war. He feared that the Gestapo might make the connection from son to father, but luckily they never did.

In March 1944 radio operators were in extremely short supply in F Section and I asked George if he would care to come on another mission with me. On reflection he said that, provided I could assure him of an unlimited quantity of cigarettes, he would be happy to accompany me. I assured him that I would do my best.

I also had news of Stargart. Angel had successfully guided him over the Pyrenees. The group of ex-prisoners from the *Maison Centrale* had now been vetted and had apparently volunteered for future service with the Firm. They were now being trained in the various SOE centres as future agents. The one-time prisoners looked as though they were likely to be of quite significant value to the French resistance. One day about the last week in March Colonel Buck informed me that the Sarthe was to be my new area.

⋆ ⋆ ⋆

At this point I may briefly summarize what I had learned from my own experience and those of my various friends in the resistance movement.

- By 1944 the vast majority of the French population was in sympathy with the Allied cause. They had always disliked the Germans but many of those who had not wished to commit themselves in the years to 1943 now felt the Occupation must end — one day. It would be a day in which many of them wanted to play a part. It was amazing indeed how many men and women were prepared to risk their lives and those of their families in actively helping the "resistance".
- There was a relatively small minority who had committed themselves to the world of Adolf Hitler — oppression, racism and domination by force. These were the adherents of the Vichy régime — some, but not all, Government officials and members of the Gendarmerie, the *Milice* and the paid informers of the Gestapo. Many of the Resistance organizations which over the years had spontaneously sprung up in France had been infiltrated by these, their members arrested and either deported or executed.
- Working independently of the large French groups, F Section agents, after the initial parachute drop, ran only the smallest of risks. This increased as the square of the number of persons involved in the organization! It might only be a matter of time before they were infiltrated or in some other way came to the notice of the Gestapo.

- An almost greater danger than that of infiltration by enemies was the gossiping of friends — and the friends of friends!
- It was imperative that, even in its early stages, a Resistance organization be divided into watertight compartments. If one compartment were infiltrated or destroyed the others must not be endangered. No one member should know anything about any of the others which it was not essential that he or she should know.
- Weapons and explosives must be dispersed in hidden caches within the area of operation. The caches should be known only to the groups which might need the material.
- Under interrogation and torture by the Gestapo no man or woman could be relied on not to give everything away. At most they might hold out for twenty-four hours. Those who were connected in any way with him or her must take action to disappear without trace with the very minimum of delay. It was a fact which was faced with marvellous courage by many of those French members of the Resistance that their families, farms and businesses made it impossible for them simply to disappear. Once they had been given away they were completely at the mercy of the Gestapo. Such was the case of M and Mme Néraud in Clermont Ferrand. It will be remembered that they used the No. 37 Rue Blatin as a safe house for Brian, George and myself immediately after our drop. It appeared that they had

continued to live at their flat in the Rue Blatin whilst managing to help Brian and George in the build-up of their organization. They were arrested by the Gestapo sometime in 1943 and were never seen again.

CHAPTER FIVE

Back to France

I did not get off to a good start as far as my activities in the Département de la Sarthe were concerned. I was staying with my aunt near Eastbourne at the end of March 1944, more or less commuting to the F Section office in London. In the interests of security we were strictly forbidden to take any papers or maps out of the office. However, I thought I would disobey this rule so as to give myself time to study what was to be my operational area. I placed my documents in a briefcase, travelled down to Haywards Heath, thought I saw the train to Eastbourne standing at another platform, rushed across to it, forgetting my briefcase, found it was the wrong train, rushed into the original train (which was via Brighton) — and found my briefcase! I was not relishing a meeting with Colonel Buck and telling him that not only had I taken secret papers out of the office but lost them as well!

On Good Friday all was ready. With George and me was also to be dropped another radio operator, Muriel Byck, code-named Michelle. She was to join up with Philippe de Vômecourt who, on account of a damaged leg, could not be dropped by parachute and had to be

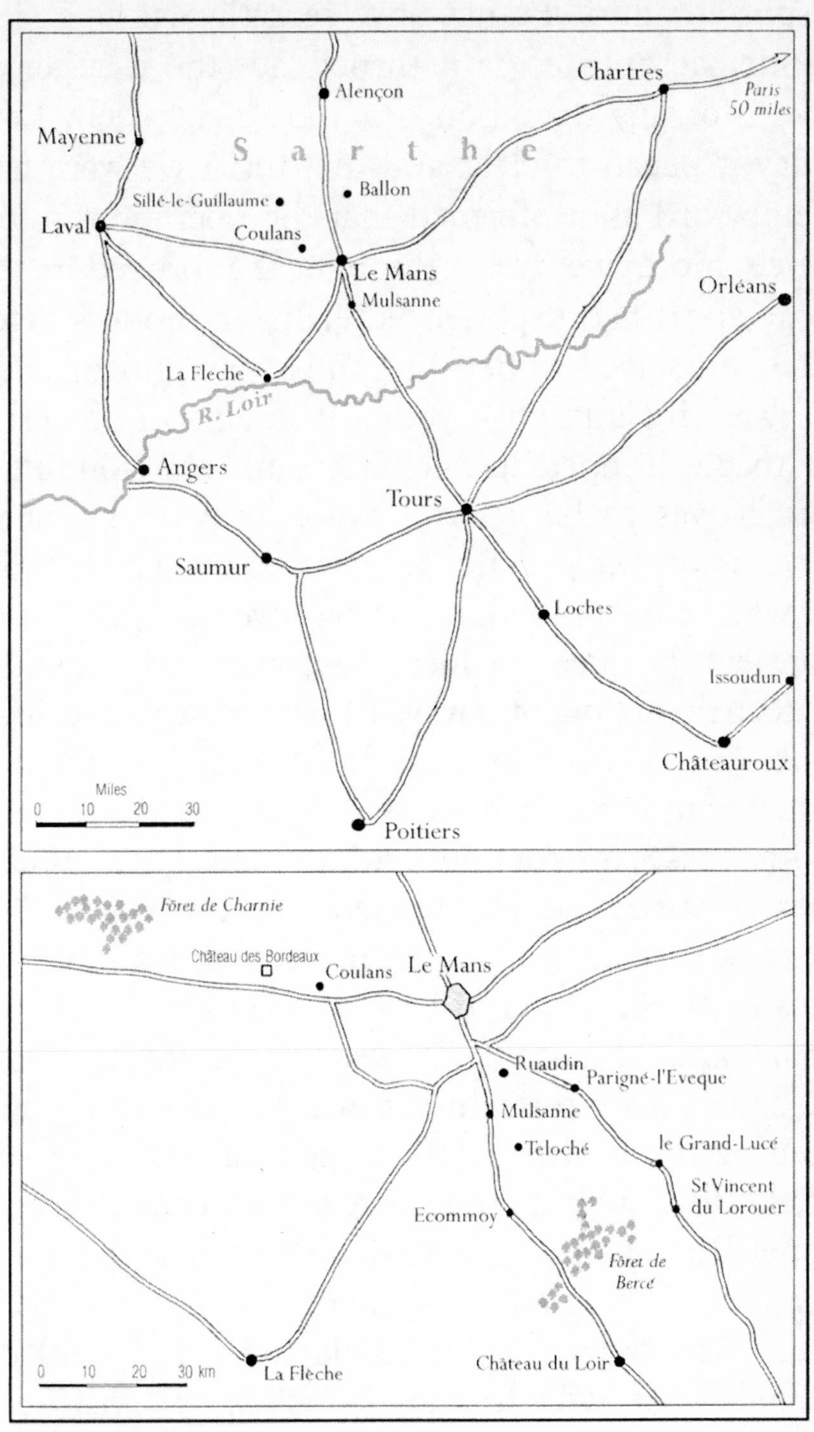
Chartres
Paris
50 miles
Alençon
Mayenne
Sarthe
Ballon
Sillé-le-Guillaume
Laval
Coulans
Le Mans
Mulsanne
Orléans
La Fleche
R. Loir
Angers
Tours
Saumur
Loches
Issoudun
Châteauroux
Miles
0 10 20 30
Poitiers
Fôret de Charnie
Château des Bordeaux
Coulans
Le Mans
Ruaudin
Parigné-l'Eveque
Mulsanne
Teloché
le Grand-Lucé
St Vincent
du Lorouer
Ecommoy
Fôret de
Bercé
0 10 20 30 km
La Flèche
Château du Loir

transported into France by secretly landing in a Lysander aeroplane. As it turned out the weather was too bad for any operation on Good Friday. On Easter Sunday it began to clear and that night we were taken to Tempsford and informed that the operation was on.

Once more we went through the procedure that George and I had experienced eighteen months before. We felt ourselves to be old hands now and of course there was this attractive young woman to impress! We were to be dropped just to the south of Issoudun. As before it was to be a blind drop, i.e. with no one to receive us on the ground. Afterwards we were to make our way into Issoudun where we would contact "Monsieur Jacques", a local contractor. He would be able to help us on our way, Muriel to a house in the neighbourhood of Tours and George and me to a country manor about 15 kms west of Le Mans.

With these instructions came several more code-names — our réseau was named "Headmaster" (all the F Section réseaux were named after professions). The names by which I was to be known in the "field" were "Albin" and "Simon". (It was important to change code-names if we thought the one we were using might be getting too well known!) As part of our cover story Muriel and I were supposed to be sister and brother. Colonel Buck and Vera Atkins wished us well from the F Section office at No. 5 Orchard Court.

Our aeroplane was a Lockheed. It included a refinement by which the parachutists, instead of dropping through a hole in the floor, sat behind one another on a kind of slide and tobogganed out into space.

Our flight was uneventful and it did not seem long before the dispatcher ordered us on to the slide, George first, Muriel second and then me. He took the cover off the trap door. The plane circled once or twice. The red light went on. I vaguely remember thinking that somehow I wasn't as nervous as I had been on the first occasion, even though we were landing this time in German-occupied territory.

Then the red light turned to green. "Go," shouted the dispatcher. George tobogganed for an instant down the slide and was gone. "Go." Muriel, without a moment's hesitation, followed. "Go," and it was my turn. Again the slipstream struck me with dizzying force. I felt the chute open and then I quietly drifted down.

Instead of the open field we were expecting, we landed in a wood. Fortunately the trees were well spaced out and none of the chutes got entangled in the branches. We had lost sight of each other and of the packages which had been dropped after us. It was not long before I found Muriel. She was already folding her chute. I kissed her and well remember her face in the moonlight. She had an expression as though to say, "That's quite nice but aren't you making rather a fuss?" Soon George joined us — it was a case of déjà-vu from 1942 — then we began hunting for the packages, including of course the vital radio. It took us some time but to our great relief we found them all. We then carried them to a particularly thick part of the wood and covered them with all the leaves and branches we could find.

All this had taken some time. We knew, however, that curfews from about 11p.m. to 6a.m. were now in force in much if not all of France. We munched an iron ration of some kind and as dawn was breaking decided to make our way to Issoudun. Venturing out of the wood, making sure that we were not being watched, we soon came to a road. We had some difficulty in pinpointing our position on the map. (I should explain that all available maps were Michelin road maps. Excellent maps but showing no ground contours.) We decided to go north. This in fact turned out to be the right direction and by around 8a.m. we found ourselves entering Issoudun. It was Easter Monday, there was not a German in sight and the local population seemed not to have heard that there was a war on! People were strolling around in the spring sunshine, apparently without a care in the world. We entered a café, ordered coffee (acorn of course) and tried to appear as inconspicuous as possible. We soon relaxed when it was clear that the other people in the café took no notice of us whatever. To George and I who had had much the same experience eighteen months before in Clermont Ferrand, it seemed astonishing that so little was to be seen of the German occupation. I noticed also another interesting point; the presence of Muriel was a considerable advantage in enabling us to fade into the background. The very presence of a girl gave a kind of normality to our little group.

It was now about ten o'clock. We moved to another café and then I left the other two and went in search of Monsieur Jacques at the address which I had been given. I found the street, with the assistance of a friendly local, then went along it looking for the number. I found it, rang the bell and asked for Monsieur Jacques. He was a large jolly man, of Alsatian origin. (I later discovered that his real name, which he obviously did not like using, was Trommelschlager!) He was a contractor by profession and possessed a large yard neighbouring the house. He had been briefed that we were coming. Quickly I fetched Muriel and George.

That evening Jacques, one of his men and George went to the place where we had concealed the packages. They took a truck with some kind of official authorization stuck on its windscreen. However, they encountered no difficulties and George quickly located the two radio sets — his own and Muriel's.

The following day I went by train to Châteauroux. My identity card and documents were better prepared than when I had confronted the Inspecteurs of the Clermont Ferrand police! However, there was only a perfunctory check when I took my ticket. I had the address of the safe house where Philippe de Vômecourt should be staying after he had been landed by Lysander. It will be remembered that he had a leg injury on the night the three of us had been dropped. I was relieved to find that all had gone well. He was now making arrangements to use an especially secure — and comfortable — safe house on a large estate near Tours belonging to a Madame Sevenet. I would go back to

Issoudun where I was certain Jacques could arrange a car. In a couple of days I would accompany Muriel and her radio set to the house of Madame Sevenet where Philippe would be waiting for us.

Nothing easier! We took a car belonging to a Jacques connection with a driver who was in the know. We picked a route which would take us away from any towns and large villages and set off about five days after our drop. The car, like all cars in France in those days, was run on charcoal or wood. The gas produced from heating either of these fuels was quite effective. The only difficulty was in getting the engine started — this was indeed a task for an expert! Also you couldn't break any speed records!

The whole trip went quite smoothly. We found Madame Sevenet's house — it was close to Loches — thanks to Philippe's careful instructions. There was one matter which I found rather worrying. Muriel, who had seemed in excellent form during the plane journey and drop and the subsequent days in Issoudun, seemed all at once to become very seedy on the car trip. She looked pale and in some kind of pain. I thought this might be the result of the journey. I was very glad to see the attentive care which Madame Sevenet and her housekeeper gave to Muriel when I took her to the back door of the house. We said a very quick goodbye. Although there seemed to be no one in sight it seemed wiser that we should get on the road back to Issoudun as soon as possible. We had arranged that I would stop off at Madame Sevenet's house when I left Issoudun for good on my way to the Sarthe. We had no trouble with the return journey and spent the evening discussing various plans with George and Jacques.

The next day we had a scare. It seemed the Germans had got wind of something and were systematically searching some of the houses in the area in which Jacques's house stood. I admit to being in a bit of a panic, wondering how we might conceal the radio set. We might bury it perhaps? We eventually stowed it away in the loft of one of the sheds. However, it was all for nothing. The Germans must have been looking for something else and Jacques's house was undisturbed. We agreed that George would stay put for the time being.

It was about a week after the drop that I mounted a bicycle — again provided by Jacques, said goodbye to the people who had helped us so much and took the country roads to Loches. Again all was peaceful. The day was very hot and after I had cycled about 70 kms, with some 20 kms remaining, I was absolutely overcome with thirst. There was a farmhouse just off the road and I approached a middle-aged woman who was near the front door. "Madame," I said, "Do you think I might have a glass of water?" "We don't drink water here," she said, "but you are welcome to some cider." She made me sit down and poured a glass. Chatting amiably about the weather I drank it. She poured another glass — and another, beautiful stuff, cool and refreshing. After the fourth glass I thanked the woman for her kindness and got on my bicycle in fine form. After about 2 kms the cider really began to work! Unable to go any further I went a little way off the road, lay down under a tree and fell fast asleep for about two hours. I woke up, rather surprisingly, without a headache and finished the last 20 kms or so to Loches and Madam Sevenet's house. Muriel had already left with Philippe and apparently had already established contact with the Firm.

I stayed that night and then went on my way to the Sarthe. I had expected that the bridges over the Loire might have some kind of control on them but none was to be seen. In Tours I happened to squeeze my bicycle rather close to a parked car. I saw a policeman eyeing me in a rather disagreeable way but happily he took no action!

About midday I stopped at a rather shabby restaurant and, using my ration card, ate some kind of sandwich. Sitting at the next table were three or four German soldiers and a middle-aged Frenchwoman. She had apparently lived in Germany for some time, in Karlsruhe, and she just adored the Germans. I was the spectator of the repellent spectacle of the smarming creature's admiration for the soldiers — who seemed quite pleasant fellows incidentally — finished my sandwich and left. Later on in the afternoon, feeling rather hungry, I stopped at a farm and asked the farm-lady whether she might have (not cider!) eggs to sell. "Certainly, Monsieur." I bought six, sat down in a field and, piercing the top and the bottom sucked them all dry. I no longer felt hungry! In the late afternoon I found my way to the address I had been given at the Château des Bordeaux. I had arrived in my area at last. Now I would really have to get down to business.

The owner of the Château des Bordeaux was a young bachelor named Edmond Cohin. In addition to the Château, Edmond was the proprietor of extensive lands surrounding it, including quite a bit of forest. He was also in touch with various other landowners and farmers throughout the Département of the Sarthe. From my briefing by Buck and Vera, I knew that SOE had already had a widespread organization in Northern France which included the Sarthe. It had been headed by an agent whose code-name was Prosper. Apparently this organization had been infiltrated by the Gestapo, resulting in a large number of arrests. Anyone connected with Prosper was to be avoided at all costs.

It was many years afterwards that I realized just how catastrophic the collapse of the Prosper *réseau* and other groups more or less connected with it had been. Several SOE agents had been arrested, among them Major Suttill, the overall leader of the whole organization, and his radio operator, Noor Inayat Khan (later awarded the George Cross). They were deported to concentration camps in Germany and executed there.

One day, long after these events, I was taken by friends from Le Mans to see a commemorative stele a short distance south of the town. It bore the names of over sixty French men and women who had been shot by the Germans. The date was shown as November 1943.

Not surprisingly these disasters had had a profound effect upon the whole area of the Sarthe. Those who had been executed or deported in 1943 would have been the very individuals who could have been the key elements in our operations of 1944. As it was, the lack of cadres made our task difficult, while at the same time the population as a whole had, not unnaturally, become somewhat reluctant to take the risks which had proved the undoing of many of their fellow citizens. Added to this was the encouragement which the collapse of the Prosper organization had given to the Gestapo and its fellow enemy agencies. All the more credit to those Sarthois and Sarthoises who did support us so valiantly.

I did did not, of course, know the prospective date of D-day. However, it was obvious that it would not be long delayed. My essential tasks were to build up a network of resistance activists and obtain enough weapons and explosives by parachute drops with which to equip them. Then they would need to be trained and tactically deployed. First of all we would have to install George and his radio set in a safe house from whence he could communicate with the Firm. The Château des Bordeaux would be possible but only for a strictly limited period, say two weeks. So near to Le Mans, the Gestapo would certainly be quick to operate one or more detector vans as soon as George's signals could be picked up. It was, we were instructed, vital that radio operators be kept on the move. Edmond had a friend who was prepared to fetch George by car from Issoudun. All went well and it was not long before George was able to set up his radio in the neighbourhood of the Château and our contact with Buck and his office was assured.

One of the contiguous properties of the Château des Bordeaux belonged to Maître Choplain (farmers in the Sarthe were always entitled Maître). He was a veteran of the First World War, had been wounded and had been decorated with the *Medaille Militaire*. Maître Choplain had a strong-looking son and a couple of nephews. The family was totally against the Boches. The son, Marcel, and his cousins would certainly be very useful in the handling of heavy containers. We enjoyed a very pleasant existence in the Château des Bordeaux; the rooms had marvellous views over the grounds and, an even greater privilege, there were mounds of butter and cream cheese on the table for breakfast every morning — this at a time when strict rationing was the rule in France! Most of the population were obliged to have recourse to the black market in order to survive. Only the farmers flourished.

It was about the beginning of May that we had our first parachute drop. The whole operation went perfectly. First a code message was broadcast on the BBC: "*L'oncle Bob mange la crème*". This was to notify us that the drop was to be expected the following night. At midnight several of us went out into a field, part of Edmond's property, and listened for the sound of a plane. Sure enough, at around one o'clock, we heard it. As part of SOE training there was a laid-down procedure for these occasions. Three men, or women, spread themselves out along a line which the plane would follow. One other man would be at the head of the line. All four were to point electric torches in the direction of the plane when its engines became plainly audible. The pilot did not take long to spot us. He circled once and then flew along the line of torches to release the parachutes with their containers. The torches were switched off and the sound of the plane's engines receded rapidly in the distance. We then proceeded to load the containers on to a couple of Maître Choplain's farm carts — very heavy they were too — and take them triumphantly to the Château. The next day we kept a sharp look out for members of the Gestapo or the French gendarmerie who might have been alerted by the sound of a plane — after all we were less than 20 kms from Le Mans — but nothing happened.

The containers held enough Sten guns and explosives to equip a small army. We hid them in the grounds and outbuildings of the Château.

Edmond's housekeeper and gardener were instructed that whenever one or other of us was out a duster should be prominently displayed at a window of the main building. If it were taken in it would be a signal that something was wrong. (The contrary procedure — to hang out a duster if unwanted visitors were in the house — would be much more likely to arouse suspicion.) It was about this time that George (he had not yet moved to another safe house) and I, as a precautionary measure, took to sleeping in tents in the woods which surrounded the Château on two sides. If a duster was on display we would come in for breakfast.

From this time I began to follow various contacts with four objects in view:

- To find one, or more, safe houses for George and his radio transmitter.
- To find other dropping grounds which would preferably be somewhat further from Le Mans than the Château des Bordeaux.
- To recruit persons capable of armed action against the Germans or of hiding and supporting those who were. To train and arm these.
- To discover one or more areas where it might be possible to establish an armed camp (a "*maquis*" as it was termed) which could be defended against the Germans and to which weapons could be freely parachuted.

In the absence of a *maquis* we would need farms where our groups could hide up when the time came for action. The town of Le Mans was obviously a major centre of communication for the German army. We should try and organize units of Resistance which would be able to ambush roads and cut telephone lines in as many directions, radiating from the town, as possible. The railways had already been destroyed by the Allied air forces and by Resistance teams operating over the last months.

A strange and sad episode took place only about a couple of weeks after we had been living at the Château. George came into our living/working room looking unusually serious. He said that Buck had sent a message telling us that Muriel (the companion of our drop) had died suddenly, apparently of some kind of heart failure. Philippe had informed him through another radio operator. It seemed incredible — only three weeks before she had jumped by parachute, apparently unruffled, into enemy-occupied territory. A few days later I was listening in my tent to the BBC coded radio messages. In addition to the usual mixture of coded nonsense phrases suddenly I heard our code names, "*Michelle pense à son frère Simon*". Muriel must have sent the message shortly before she died and the BBC had just transmitted it along with all the others. I was devastatingly touched by this incident and the memory of this courageous, attractive British-French-Jewish girl, whom I had only known for a few days, has remained with me ever since.

By the second week in May our organization was growing rapidly. I was able to contact a number of farmers and local businessmen. We received another drop of arms. Delighted as I was with the way in which the citizens of the Sarthe were rallying to the Allied cause, I was under no illusion that, in an area so near the north coast of France, the Gestapo would not be particularly sensitive to any kind of subversive activity, let alone armed resistance to the German occupation. I endeavoured, as far as I could, to keep our embryo Resistance groups separate from each other. At least if one or other were infiltrated or given away the remainder might not be incriminated. I was well aware of the danger of gossip. "Do you know what happened last night? There was a parachute drop in the field next door! Don't tell anybody, will you?" and so on until it got to the long ears of a Gestapo informer. One particular problem was what to do with the parachute canopies. The French women, deprived of textiles for so long years, were excruciatingly tempted to make blouses out of the beautiful nylon material. To succumb would make the proud wearers liable to immediate arrest! I had been told in training that nylon could be burnt. One attempt to do so in the fireplace of the Château des Bordeaux resulted in a thick black liquid spreading out on the floor, much to the dismay of Edmond's housekeeper. In the end we packed them tightly and sank them under a bridge over a kind of moat at the front of the château. On other occasions the parachutes were buried.

Around the middle of May I felt the need for some assistance. I sent a message to Buck and his staff asking for a capable organizer and for a girl courier. I felt that a girl could pass unnoticed in the town or the countryside much more easily than could a man and on other occasions could accompany me when visiting our contacts in Le Mans. As I have said, I had noticed from my very brief stay in Issoudun that going about in the town with Muriel enabled George or me to fade into the background with surprising ease.

Shortly afterwards a rather alarming event took place. We were scheduled to have an arms drop somewhere south-west of Le Mans at perhaps 30–35 kms from the town. We had selected a good field, well away from any habitations. The code message had been passed by the BBC and around midnight the men proceeded to align themselves with their torches according to the procedure which had worked very satisfactorily on at least two occasions. We heard the sound of the plane rapidly approaching, the torches were switched on and we confidently awaited the plane to pass overhead discharging the containers with their parachutes as it went. We saw it dark against the moonlight, preparing, as we thought, for the final run in — then to our absolute dismay we saw the parachutes floating down, perhaps three or four kilometres away. We made our way as rapidly as possible to the area where the containers and the 'chutes were spread all over the place. There were about twelve of them, each requiring two or three men to handle them. We did not have the farm carts which we were to have used on the original dropping ground. Worst of all we were on the outskirts of a village. It was amazing that none of the inhabitants was yet on the spot. The situation was hopeless and we quickly decided to abandon the containers and get away as rapidly as possible. We returned to our various farms and safe-houses more than disappointed. The next day the wife of one of our members, looking out of the window of her house, saw a couple of German army trucks piled high with our containers. If the Gestapo had not been alerted before, they certainly were now. In any case it would now become more important than ever for us to keep separate the various elements of our steadily growing organization.

It was not long before the Firm reacted to our request for assistance. We were informed that two men and a woman would be dropped, together with a number of containers, on the night of 28-29 May. The location which we had indicated was appreciably further from Le Mans than on previous occasions, not far from La Flèche. I did not go to the drop myself as I was tied up with some recruitment activity the evening of the day before. Early in the morning of the 29th I bicycled to the safe house in the neighbourhood of La Flèche where I knew the agents and the containers from the previous night's drop were being temporarily housed. I was welcomed by the leader of the "reception committee", as the team on the dropping ground was termed. He told me that some of the containers and packages had gone astray and possibly been picked up by the Germans whose transport was using a road at a considerable distance from the dropping ground. One of the agents had been taken into hiding at a nearby farm, together with some of the weapons and explosives. The other two agents, a man and a woman, were waiting for me in the next room.

The "host", if one may call him that, accompanied me to a room where the agents were waiting. I saw a strong-looking young man whom I already knew quite well and an extremely pretty girl whom I had seen, and noticed with some appreciation, in one or other of the offices of the Firm. In view of the vital role that these two persons were to play in the development of the resistance in the Sarthe, I think I should give some details of their previous careers.

Raimond Glaesner (often known as Kiki) was a native of Alsace. In addition to French, he was bilingual in German as well as in the Alsatian dialect (which, as he confidently told us, neither a Frenchman nor a German could understand!). An adventurous character, he was aged about twenty-four when he began wondering whether he should enlist in the French *Milice* which was fighting alongside the German troops in the battles on the Russian front, or he thought, perhaps he might join the French Resistance. One day he was walking along the street of his native Saarlouis he encountered a German who pushed him off the pavement. Raimond reacted by hitting the man in the face and racing off at top speed. He decided that the Resistance would suit him better than the Russian front and rapidly became involved in one of the entirely French-based organizations. Some of these were dangerously exposed to penetration by the collaborators of the Gestapo and in the summer of 1943 Raimond found himself imprisoned in the *Maison Centrale d'Eysses*. For some reason he was allocated to the *Quartier Disciplinaire*. Philippe and I quickly spotted him as a useful potential recruit for SOE. He participated in our escape and in the subsequent crossing of the Pyrenees. I lost sight of him when we left Gibraltar. Now here he was, with a spell of SOE training behind him.

Sonia d'Artois (known, amongst a variety of other names, as Blanche and Madeleine) was the daughter of an RAF Group Captain. She had been mostly educated in France and spoke French as a native. Her services background was WAAF and then, on volunteering for SOE, had become a FANY, as were all the female agents of the Firm. She had passed through a number of training schools and shortly before dropping into the

Sarthe, had married Guy d'Artois, a Canadian officer and also an SOE agent.

The reader may wonder about my personal relationship with this young woman with whom I was to share some rather searing experiences. I will briefly recount two episodes which may make the matter clear.

In the course of my SOE training I recall that one of the members of my class asked the lecturer, Jerry Morell, how the Firm felt about female agents. He said, "In our experience women are more brave, more loyal and more resourceful than men." In the second episode, about 50 years later, I was discussing a TV documentary about SOE with the producer. He had seen the portraits of some of the agents which hang on the wall of the Special Forces Club in London. Suddenly he said with a curious stiffness, "I see that some of the women were rather handsome. Wasn't it difficult not to fall in love with them?" I can confirm the truth of both these pronouncements.

The third parachuted agent revealed himself as having a strong English accent in his spoken French. We were obliged to hide him in a tent in the grounds of the Château des Bordeaux until we could find something for him to do. His training had been as a weapons instructor which should surely be a useful asset later on. His name was Eugène Bec and his code-name Hugue.

We decided that Raimond would take charge of all the groups south of Le Mans and that we would move some of the arms and explosives to the safety of various farms in that area. Madeleine and I were to strengthen the organization in Le Mans itself by bringing in some local businessmen who could supply the groups with clothes and shoes and any other civilian requirements which were unobtainable except on the black market. We managed to rent a small house, No 8 Rue Mangeard, so that we need not return to the Château, a good hour by bicycle every evening.

On the morning of 6 June Madeleine was sleeping upstairs and I was installed on a sofa on the ground floor. We were awakened by the sound of bombs falling nearby. Allied bombers were targeting the railway station; in fact it had already been destroyed. Thinking that Madeleine might be frightened I dashed upstairs to her room. I need not have bothered; she was completely unperturbed. The bombardment did not last long and soon all appeared normal on the streets of the town.

I had a rendezvous with George that morning at around eleven o'clock. He told me that the Allies had landed in Normandy. The coded messages broadcast on the BBC radio ordered all SOE agents to attack or sabotage roads, telephone lines and railways (superfluous in our area). This was certainly exciting news. My first reaction was a tinge of disappointment: what a pity that we could not have had more time to improve our organization and stage more drops of arms and possibly agents. It hardly occurred to me that at the rate we were going it could only be a matter of time, shorter rather than longer, before the Gestapo would penetrate our network.

I had imagined that Le Mans being such a short distance from the Normandy front, the whole of the

Sarthe would be alive with German troops. Quite a few of us slept in tents or under tarpaulins away from villages or houses, thinking that any accommodation would be requisitioned. But, to our considerable surprise, nothing seemed to happen. The only rather alarming incident occurred when a German convoy descended without notice on the Château des Bordeaux and demanded lunch! Edmond and I were in the grounds at the time and felt sure that the Germans, headed by a General or Colonel, would requisition the entire property. Fortunately the containers of arms and explosives had nearly all been distributed. However, enough remained in the grounds of the Château that, if discovered, we would be in serious trouble indeed. We managed to whisper to Edmond's housekeeper through a window at the back of the kitchen that the Germans should be provided with the finest lunch possible, with plenty of wine and Calvados (the local and very potent apple brandy, 40% alcohol) and to drag out the proceedings as much as possible. In the meantime Edmond and I, aided by two or three member of the Choplain family, carried the incriminating items — Sten guns, radio set, batteries and tents with our personal belongings — into a dense wood, which was not part of the actual property of the Château, some three-quarters of a kilometre away. When the Germans had finished their protracted and sumptuous lunch, they did not requisition the Château but said "Thank you" to the housekeeper and her assistant and continued on their way.

It was about the middle of June that I received a visit at the Château from a young man, Jehan de la Rochefordière, who had made contact via a neighbouring organization. He came to see me at the Château. Although we were sleeping in the grounds at the time, we used to come in to the Château to eat the excellent breakfast Edmond's housekeeper prepared for us. Jehan recalls that I invited him to breakfast just as we were distributing some containers of arms and explosives. It appears that I was "very friendly". Jehan also commented on the good looks of my secretary (sic). He remembers that I refused to give his organization any arms, saying something to the effect that we knew that all non-F Section Resistance organisations were already infiltrated by the Gestapo. On his return to his headquarters, somewhere north of Orlèans, he found that my prognosis had been all too true. All his companions had been arrested. He himself was taken into custody, but later released as there was no trace of his complicity with the Resistance. He had, moreover, an excellent cover story that he was an inspector of woodland forests.

It was surprising how once the Normandy front had to some extent stabilized and it had become clear that the Allies were not on course for an immediate breakthrough, life began to return to normal again. There was certainly more German military activity than before but little in the way of restrictions on the movement of civilians. We were particularly anxious to produce some action, however little it might be, which would contribute something to the hard-pressed Allied armies, fighting against desperate German counter-attacks, to secure the beachheads on the coast.

For a short time we established a *maquis* — a band of armed men living in a forest, either regularly on the move and avoiding contact with the Germans or, if they were strong enough, able to defend themselves against any attack the Germans could launch at them. It was led by Raimond. However, it was found that, though the *maquis*, which at the time consisted of about thirty men, could perhaps maintain itself, the need for continuously being on guard simply took up too many men. Added to this were the problems of finding and transporting food.

All in all, we decided that we would disperse the *maquis* into a number of small groups of four or five men. These could be hidden in friendly farms of which we had quite a number, well dispersed around the southern approaches to Le Mans. It was thought, probably rather a faint hope, that if the Germans traced the men, mostly young, to a farm, they might be able to pose as *réfractaires*, i.e. persons who were evading conscription into German industry. All the groups were under the rather tenuous command of Raimond who held responsibility for the supply of weapons and explosives. The objectives of the groups were to ambush German convoys on the roads leading to Le Mans from the south. The ambushes took place at night and the groups concerned would be well under cover by daylight, usually in a farm at some distance from the place of the ambush.

At this point I should perhaps describe the usual technique by our groups used to cause as much damage to the Germans as possible, with the minimum of danger to themselves.

The location would be in a forest or thick wood on a main road. There would be a track or country road nearby, but not leading to the main road, to allow the ambushers to escape by running through the trees and bushes and then mounting bicycles — at least one group had a car and a driver waiting for it. On the arrival of the German convoy the ambushers would open up on the leading truck with Sten guns and, as it ran into a ditch, rake any other vehicles with fire, hurl some grenades and make off before the element of surprise began to evaporate. Sometimes one or more German motorcyclists would pass by. These were easy targets for the Sten guns.

We knew that there could be other Resistance groups operating in the Sarthe, but, sadly, by the summer of 1944 the Gestapo had managed to arrest most of these brave men and women, and ours was almost certainly the only organization capable of armed activities.

Closer to Le Mans was another of our networks, led by three brothers, Hillaret by name, and yet another, directed by a rather flamboyant character, Claude Hureau.

We also had to find a hide-out for three RAF aircraftsmen who had been picked up by some friendly farmer. Their plane had been severely damaged over northern France but they had been able to parachute out of it before it crashed. Most pressing of all was the constant need to move George and his radio set before the German detector service was able to pinpoint the source of his transmissions — also to provide him with, at least, some cigarettes!

All these ramifications for our organization necessitated another supply drop of arms. George transmitted the message to the Firm and it was not long before our coded message was broadcast by the BBC. The drop took place somewhere to the south-west of Le Mans about the beginning of July and this time there was no hitch. About a dozen containers of arms were safely received, together with a sum of money. I should explain that since the abortive attempt to form a *maquis*, the members of our networks were living more or less lives of daytime normality. Those of us who were in or near the town of Le Mans, for instance, applied for our monthly ration cards — not too difficult provided one's identity card would pass a cursory check — and bought such necessities of life as were available in the shops. There was little enough to be had and increasingly we made use of the black market. Occasionally after a hard day bicycling on various missions, organizing supplies, advising and co-ordinating the activities of our groups, Madeleine and I would take our dinner at a black market restaurant just out of town. It was much favoured by German officers. The food was quite good and the proprietress did not ask for ration cards. She obviously regarded us as "collaborators" and became quite friendly.

Hugue was able to accompany some of the members of the local group on missions which targeted telephone lines, cutting the overhead wires or digging up underground cables.

Our organization, although still effectively separated into autonomous groups, was growing so fast that I decided that we must try to form another *maquis*. This might comprise some fifty men and would enable us to received parachute drops with more arms and possibly SOE agents to provide training and leadership. The best place we could find was the Forêt de Charnie. This is quite a large area of forest situated about 40 kms west of Le Mans in the direction of Laval. Obviously the Germans would be particularly sensitive to any form of military operation in their rear approaches to the Normandy front. Nevertheless there seemed a good possibility that, once established, organized and armed, a sizeable group of men would be able to carry out damaging attacks against German units based in the neighbourhood of Le Mans. Their mobility within the forest would make it difficult for the Germans to pinpoint their whereabouts. George and his radio set would also be based on the *maquis*.

Anything that we could do to distract the Germans from their operations on the Normandy front must help the Allies, if only by the smallest margin. As of early July, their advance seemed to be held in check. It was impossible to know for how long.

CHAPTER
SIX

The Gestapo Strikes

The first phase of "Operation Charnie" was to bring together all the groups west of Le Mans. Edmond was to be in charge. George and his radio set went with him, together with Eugène who should now be increasingly useful as a weapons instructor. In guerrilla warfare his accent would not be a problem. All this activity proceeded surprisingly smoothly. Soon about twenty-five men were settled in tents or under tarpaulins in the forest. The local villagers supplied them with food. They were already provided with arms from some of the previous drops. The Germans were nowhere to be seen.

The second phase was to add more men to the *maquis* and to carry out more drops of arms. A young man, code-named Philippe, had a connection with a potential resistance group in the area of Sillé-le-Guillaume. He visited the Charnie and agreed that his men, about ten in number, would join Edmond and those who were already there. To those could be added the three RAF aircraft men who had baled out. They should be better in the *maquis* than in the farm where they now were. They could also prove useful in handling weapons. It was agreed with Philippe that he and the thirteen other men would join those in the Charnie on the night of 5–6 July.

At the same time we felt that the *maquis* of the Charnie was now sufficiently settled to receive an arms drop. George informed the Firm that this was the case. Our code message to be broadcast by BBC in the course of *"quelques messages personels"* was to be *"le chacal mange les chevaux"*. Sure enough the "Beeb" carried our message on the evening of 6 July and all was set for the night of the seventh. It was my intention to go to the Charnie on the eighth, assist in the general organization of the developing *maquis* and prepare its future plan of operations. Madeleine would go with me to Charnie and then return immediately to Le Mans. She had now become our de facto administrative officer, although the Firm always entitled its women agents (other than radio operators) "couriers". Her work involved the distribution of arms and explosives, also, on occasion, instructing the *résistants* in their use, making contacts "through friends of friends" and recruiting other, potentially useful individuals into our *réseau*.

On the morning of the seventh came disquieting news. Philippe and his group, including the RAF men, had been expected the preceding night but had not turned up. Shortly afterwards we heard that the Germans had arrested some men on one of the roads leading from Sillé-le-Guillaume. By now the Gestapo would certainly be alerted to the fact that something was going on in the forest of the Charnie. However, we could do nothing to postpone the drop.

I set out with Madeleine, as planned, on the morning of the eighth. When we reached the Château des Bordeaux we called in at Maître Choplain's farm. We found his wife in a state of despair. From what she said the Germans must have already attacked the *maquis* and probably destroyed it.

From various sources we were rapidly able to piece together what had happened. Philippe, under a succession of beatings, must have guided a company of German soldiers to the exact location of the *maquis*, where the men were preparing for the drop of containers. The surprise appeared to be total. However, two men, Eugene Bec and Claude Hillaret, seized their Sten guns and by sacrificing their lives managed to hold off the German soldiers until most of the others were able to scatter. Some men were taken prisoner. Edmond and George had succeeded in escaping but the precious radio set had gone. Fortunately, without George, the Gestapo would be unable to make use of it. To make matters worse, the Germans had manned the dropping ground in the cutting in the forest. They apparently had information as to the SOE procedures and had flashed torches at the low-flying planes. As a result they managed to receive all the arms intended for the *maquis* — two planeloads of containers.

Edmond and George made their way to a farm about 10 kms from the Charnie where Edmond had a contact. On the way George took the opportunity to bury all the radio codes which, fortunately, he always carried on his person. From the farm Edmond was able to notify me as to his whereabouts.

Before returning to Le Mans Madeleine and I managed to contact the farmhouse, only a few kilometres from the Château des Bordeaux, where Edmond and George had managed to take refuge. Not surprisingly, the farmer and his wife were extremely nervous about taking them in, insisting on their being out of the house itself most of the time in a kind of back garden. They feared that the Gestapo would follow up its success in the Charnie by searching every house for kilometres around. We assured them that we would be back the following day with two more bicycles and take Edmond and George away, both of whom were badly shaken by what had happened.

We returned to Le Mans absolutely shattered. However, one incident stands out in my mind. At the entrance to Le Mans on the west side is quite a long and relatively steep slope. About halfway down was a gateway leading to some property which had been requisitioned by the Germans. Lounging about half into the main road was a sentry in Wehrmacht uniform.

Suddenly I saw Madeleine accelerate her bicycle and at top speed she made straight for the soldier. He just had an instant to step back. It gave me a short pulse of encouragement.

The following day we made the return journey with two extra bicycles to collect Edmond and George. As I was loading them onto the bus to take them the first 20 kms, the driver, whom I had often seen when travelling between the Château and the town, suddenly said,

"Where do you come from, Monsieur? You're not French." Maybe he had been alerted by events in the Charnie. As calmly as I could I replied, "What do you think? But I'm from the east." (Implying I might be from Alsace-Lorraine). His face fell and he looked quite disappointed. We brought the four bicycles to the farm in which Edmond and George were sheltering in the back yard.

We bade a rather terse farewell to the farmer and his wife and set off for the untouched part of our organization in the southern part of the Department of the Sarthe. After a few kilometres one of the tyres of my bicycle punctured irreparably. Madeleine took Edmond and George on the rest of the journey whilst I pushed my bicycle some 15 kms to Le Mans. I arrived in a general state of depression such as I have rarely experienced.

As a result of the attack on the *maquis* of the Charnie, we had lost three cars, one million francs, and a large amount of parachuted material. The men were dispersed or deported and the population of the area, once so co-operative, had now become almost hostile. It was reliably reported that fifteen Germans, including their commander, had been killed during the attack.

The following day Madeleine returned to Le Mans. She confirmed that Edmond and George had now been safely accommodated in one of the more remote farms. She had been able to talk to Raimond and to one of the other group leaders in the southern Sarthe. It appeared that our security had held firm and that there had been no repercussions from the disaster in the Charnie. It was, nevertheless, a disaster, for which I felt I carried the full responsibility. No matter what activities I might have been engaged in I should have been present in the *maquis* in its formative stages. I should also have foreseen that the Germans would do their utmost to eliminate such a large and dangerous body of men as the *maquis* in Charnie might have become, so close to the Normandy front. On the other hand, if Philippe and his group had not chanced into a German patrol, if he had managed to resist beatings and torture, even for a day or two, above all if the *maquis* had had even a little time to develop, if they had been able to increase their mobility in the depths of the forest, if, if if . . . Well, we had to face the reality of events and adjust our tactics accordingly.

Something needed to be done to restore morale and that curious sense of leadership which the SOE agents provided and without which the whole organization would probably founder. One may well consider what follows to be an act of pure foolishness or of unjustifiable frivolity.

The Restaurant des Ifs (now no longer in existence) before the War had been the favourite haunt of the drivers participating in the *24 Heures du Mans*.

Now its customers were senior German officers, possibly with a sprinkling of collaborators. Madeleine and I decided that this would be just the place for us to have a little black-market dinner. We smartened ourselves as far as we could (Madeleine looked as pretty as ever and I shaved and put on a clean shirt) and presented ourselves to the head waiter at the

Restaurant des Ifs. "We have no table free at the moment," he said. "But if Monsieur and Madame would care to share?" "But of course!" He showed us to a table where a middle-aged German was sitting by himself. We greeted each other amicably. His French wasn't very good, but we managed a little friendly chatter.

It was about this time that Madeleine took part in an incident which (in retrospect) seemed rather amusing. Propping up her bicycle outside a shop in one of the streets of Le Mans, she came out to find a German soldier riding off on it. She followed him on foot and was pleased to see that he had gone into another shop, leaving the bicycle in front of it. Swiftly taking advantage of the situation, she recovered her bicycle and rode happily away.

On another occasion she saw a German woman — there were quite a few working in the authorities of the occupation — wearing a dress which seemed familiar. It had been in one of the packages which had been lost when Madeleine had parachuted in to the Sarthe at the end of May.

It was now essential to make an assessment in respect of our organization as it stood and to prepare a plan for its future. There were several points to take into consideration.

- The Allies seemed, for the time being, to be contained in the bridgehead they had managed to gain in Normandy. They would surely break out of it one day, but when would that day be?

- The Gestapo, fresh from its success in the Charnie, would be more than ever determined to eliminate the guerrilla bands which were attacking German transport and cutting the telephone lines.
- We now had no radio set for George to operate. We must endeavour to obtain one, possibly from Philippe de Vômecourt's organization. We might be able to contact him through Madame Sevenet.
- We had a sufficient supply of arms and explosives resulting from previous drops. As it happened, one useful collection had been dumped in a wood and concealed under a tarpaulin covered with bracken. A German army unit had subsequently decided to install itself in the same wood. One of our members (a former senior NCO of the French Army) posing as a farm labourer, took a horse and cart, loaded the entire dump into the cart, covered it with a tarpaulin and then gave it a further covering of manure. He confidently drove the horse and cart out of the wood, the German soldiers taking no notice of him whatever!
- In spite of the Charnie, we possessed a large network of different contacts widely spread in the southern part of the Sarthe and in Le Mans itself. This would prove invaluable in the planning and execution of future operations. It could also progressively increase the danger of infiltration or any other form of counter-attack by the Gestapo. It was to be noticed that, in the attack on the Charnie, the Gestapo must have been able to have rapid recourse to regular soldiers of the Wehrmacht.

Unless we could in some way re-establish radio communication and receive more parachute drops we must now limit ourselves to producing the maximum amount of damage to the Germans which our resources could sustain. To this end we should

- Distribute arms, explosives and particularly ammunition between as many groups as we now had. There should be no further expansion.
- Re-double our security measures.

 i. Small groups of four or five men would operate quite separately from each other.
 ii. As far as possible (there would have to be some exceptions) nobody should know where the other members of the organisation were living.
 iii. Operate as far as possible by night. Lie up in farmhouses by day.
 iv. In the town avoid being picked up after curfew,
 v. Only use code names or, at the worst, first names.

The situation was changed by the fact that, although we had arms and explosives, we had hardly any money. Our "treasury" had been captured in the Charnie. Our groups frequently lacked suitable clothes for operating in dense country at night and of course they also needed shoes and bicycle tyres. All of these were scarce indeed at the end of four years of the German Occupation and only purchasable, if at all, on the black market. In some way we had to provide ourselves with funds. Once more I had recourse to Edmond Cohin. He said that he had an uncle, the Abbé Chevalier, who was the Treasurer of the Catholic Church in the Diocese of Le Mans. He wondered whether his uncle might be able to do something for us. I must say that I doubted very much that the Church could, or would, come to our aid. However, as an uncle to Edmond it would be unlikely that the reverend gentleman would give us away to the Gestapo. I had heard that the Catholic hierarchy, though initially rather favourable to Marshal Pétain, had been by no means welcoming to the Germans in the Occupied Zone. In some cases priests had even played an active part in the Resistance. We felt that we must try our luck.

With a member of one of our groups who had some connection with the diocese of St Julien in Le Mans, Madeleine made a first approach to the Abbé Chevalier. The Abbé was non-committal, but said that he would be prepared to meet the leader of our organization.

With a brief note from Edmond which merely informed the Abbé that I was a friend, I presented myself at the door of his residence in the precinct of the Cathedral of St Julien. The Abbé, a middle-aged man in clerical dress, did not seem particularly surprised at the short description I gave him of our organization's activities, ending with a suggestion that the Diocese might come to our financial rescue. He did not turn this down but asked what assurance I could give him that the Allies would reimburse the amount to the Church when they captured Le Mans. I said that all I could do was to give him a personal note addressed to Colonel Buckmaster. He told me that he would consider the matter and to come back in three days' time.

In three days I again rang the bell of the Abbé's residence. Without further discussion, he asked me in a very businesslike way to give him whatever kind of IOU I could. I did my best and signed with my real name and code name. He gave me frs200,000 from the Church funds. It was the greatest help to our hard-pressed organization. (In time and with considerable difficulty the Abbé managed to get my IOU to Buck and was repaid in full.) He certainly risked not only the money for which he was responsible, but also a highly disagreeable encounter with the Gestapo.

Our next task was to obtain clothes and shoes. One of our members had some connections with local businessmen and I managed to get myself introduced to two, Monsieur Rousseau was the general manager of a large department store, the shelves of which, in the summer of 1944 were practically empty. The other was Monsieur Kéranflech. The latter had been closely associated with the *24 Heures du Mans* — not a particularly useful connection under the prevailing circumstances one might think. Somehow or other these two gentlemen were able to supply us with a considerable quantity of workmen's overalls and boots.

Distribution was always a problem, remembering that none of us were supposed to know where any of the others lived. We were able to establish periodic rendezvous with Raimond and through him with the other group leaders of the southern Sarthe. Here we had the help of another valiant farmer, his wife and pretty daughter. Maître Ory's farm was situated near Téloché, close enough to Le Mans but away from the main road. One way or another we quickly got the precious supplies distributed.

During this time our groups had been operating quite successfully against German convoys on the roads converging on Le Mans. Many telephone lines were cut, not only the overhead wires but, with more difficulty, the underground cables. It is to be recorded that our friend Maître Choplain, *Medaille Militaire* of the First World War, went one night with a single companion to a loop of road near Coulans, dug up the underground cable connecting Le Mans and Laval and successfully cut it. Edmond and George who by this time were installed in a safe house somewhere just north of Le Mans were able to cut a number of overhead lines which must have been connected to the German front in Normandy.

There were, I believe, other groups, not part of our organization, involved in this important task. Its importance was a secret which only emerged some time after the war. Disrupting all telephone and telegraph communication on the ground would oblige the Germans to use radio instead. At this stage of the War the Allies' cryptographers (their work was centred on Bletchley Park) had succeeded in cracking virtually all the codes used by the Wehrmacht. Obliging the Germans to use radio communication was thus tantamount to keeping Allied HQ informed of all their plans, troop movements, supplies, etc.

Then we encountered another awkward problem. It was noticed by our members living in the areas where the telephone lines had been cut that the Germans were using French Post Office linesmen to make the repairs. This problem was solved by passing a message, via contacts in the Post Office, to the effect that where the wires or cables had been cut, the ground around it would be liable to be booby-trapped. The warning — it was a bluff — seemed to have a considerable dampening effect on the enthusiasm of the Post Office linesmen to carry out speedy repairs!

In the course of July, our organization comprised the following Groups.

- Group A: Based at St Vincent du Larouet. Operating around the Forêt de Bercé. This was in the charge of Raimond Glaesner. It consisted of six sections mostly equipped with cars. They were thus able to operate at considerable distance from the various farms at which they hid up during the day. Objectives: ambushes, cutting telephone lines and cables.
- Group B: Based near Téloché. Operating in the area of Ecommoy — Le Grand-Lucé. Under the charge of Claude Hureau. It was composed of four, then five sections. Operations more difficult here because of the proximity to Le Mans.
- Objectives:- ambushes, cutting telephone lines and cables.
- Group C. This was the responsibility of George Jones, who, of course, was no longer acting as a radio-operator. The area was centred on Ballon

and was described as "thick with Germans". The group, which only consisted of half-a-dozen men, concentrated on telephone lines and cables leading north from Le Mans and which an underground source stated as being of particular importance.

- Group D. After the disaster of the Forêt de Charnie we strictly limited our operations west of Le Mans. Nevertheless Maître Choplain and his friends kept cutting the cables running from Le Mans to Laval and Rennes.
- Group E. This was a region of the Mayenne in the charge of André Druot. He already possessed some arms, but I was able to supply him with directives and money. At a greater distance from Le Mans, this group was able to carry out a number of ambushes.

CHAPTER SEVEN

Operation Post Office

It was about the first week of July that a couple of "outsiders" became the responsibility of our organization. One of them was picked up by one of our farmer friends. He turned out to be another RAF aircraftsman who had baled out of a damaged plane. I had a short talk with him. There was no question of trying to smuggle him out of German-occupied France. So we decided to put him in a safe house where he would just have to stay put for as long as the Allies took to drive through the German lines in Normandy. He knew no French whatever, but as long as he did not venture out of the house he was safe enough. We codenamed him Benjamin. Madeleine or I managed to visit him occasionally.

The other "outsider" was different. A man was picked up by yet another French farmer (not, however, one of our particular friends) in the last stages of exhaustion. The farmer gave him something to drink and eat. When he had recovered a little, he declared himself to be a Norwegian who had been conscripted into the German Army. Now he was trying to desert and was hoping to join the French Resistance. The farmer approached one of our groups, led by Claude Hureau, which had quite a number of ambushes to its credit. Claude decided to meet the Norwegian. He turned out to be an agreeable young man only waiting to find some means of getting even with the Germans for the oppression of his nation. I must admit to feeling a certain suspicion as to the authenticity of this Norwegian. Claude, however, felt that he should be allowed to prove himself. Sure enough he joined Claude's group and took part in several ambushes shooting, and even killing, German soldiers. Henceforth Claude regarded *le Norvégien* as one of his team. On hearing that somewhere in the organization was a British officer he said that he would particularly like to meet me. In spite of Claude's assurances, I continued to feel that this was a man whom I would prefer to avoid.

Certainly the number of people now associated, in one way or another, with our organization was becoming alarming. Although the security separation of our groups apparently remained intact it could only be a matter of time before this would begin to break down. It is a cardinal principle of underground or guerrilla-type warfare that the headquarters of the organization must remain intact. So long as any damage is restricted to branches or subsidiaries so long will the headquarters (or whatever it may be called) be able to create new ones, provided of course that branch security is not breached. With this principle in mind, I had the feeling that as long as Raimond, Madeleine or I were able to exert some measure of co-ordination so long would some form of resistance remain active in the Sarthe, no matter what might happen. As an extra safety measure we changed our HQ (which nobody was supposed to know about — but some did) to an even more secure house, belonging to a local businessman. I also changed my code name from Simon to Michel (Michel had been the code name of our companion, Brian Rafferty, on our first drop. He was now in the hands of the Gestapo). Michelle had been the code name of Muriel Byck and finally it was the real name of my cousin Michael Rumbold, Lieutenant RNVR, who had been killed in a mine-sweeper in 1941. Our task must be to hold on, regardless of the odds, until the Allies would break out of their foothold in Normandy. The fighting was certainly intensifying there, but how long would the Germans hold on?

If the Allies were to be held up for any length of time, say a matter of weeks or even months, it was essential that we obtain another radio set so that George could again be put in communication with Buck and the Firm. It would not be long before we would need further supplies by parachute. An attempt to contact Philippe de Vômecourt in Orléans came to nothing. We decided that Madeleine should set off on her bicycle travelling via Tours to Loches where I was able to give her the location of Madame Sevenet's house. She would stay there and try to contact Philippe or whoever might help us to a radio. It could of course either be dropped somewhere in the Sarthe, or, in the unlikely event of them having one to spare, perhaps she would be able to transport it on the grid of her bicycle!

Madeleine was a good cyclist and it would be quite possible for her to go to Loches from Le Mans in one day.

The Germans would not be placing controls on the roads leading south of Le Mans except possibly on the bridges across the Loire. A young woman with good identity papers should, in any case, not have much trouble on the way. All the same, I saw Madeleine off with some misgivings. As the days went by I became more than ever anxious as to what might have happened to her. However, there was nothing I could do.

It was about 17 July that Claude Hureau reported that one of the members of his group, Raguideau by name, whose father was a senior administrative official in the PTT (*Poste, Télégraphe et Téléphone*) had informed him that the Germans were on the very point of bringing into service a completely new distribution centre for all their telephone lines. It seemed vital that this must be destroyed. I have said that I had so far tended to keep myself in the background in spite of Raimond's invitations to take part in one or more ambushes, but I felt that the sabotage of the distribution unit was an absolutely essential operation for which I must carry direct responsibility. Claude and I must carry out the operation together.

We first discussed the situation with Monsieur Raguideau *père*. It appeared that the distributor was in an underground chamber beneath the main Post Office building and just across the street from the *Feldkommandantur*, the HQ of the German Authority for Sarthe. Monsieur Raguideau told us that by 1830 hours the place was deserted — the German watchman would be upstairs — and that it would be easy with a couple of levers to open the door of the chamber in which the distributor was situated. There was a concierge at the entrance and we were to ask for Monsieur "X", who was actually away on leave.

On 25 July Claude Hureau and I set out on our bicycles from the Rue Mangeard. We each carried a bag containing about one and a half kgs of plastic high explosive. We were to meet Monsieur Raguideau at 18.30. Punctually we were there. No sign of Monsieur Raguideau, but the concierge was on duty! We duly enquired after Monsieur "X" "He's not here." We walked, with our bicycles, round the block. A shopkeeper who had seen us pass up the street the first time looked at us suspiciously. Again no sign of Monsieur Raguideau. We decided to wait for half an hour. Claude recalls that we sat for a while on the nearby Place, originally the Place de la République, now the Place Maréchal Pétain, while a man was making an impassioned speech about the virtues of the Maréchal. Apparently I said that it was interesting! After about twenty minutes we again entered the Post Office. Monsieur Raguideau was on the lookout for us this time and he indicated that the coast was now clear and we should proceed as rapidly as possible.

We went down some steps leading to the basement of the building and then turned to our left. Facing us was the door of the room which held the distributor. This was a much more solid affair than we had understood from Monsieur Raguideau's description. The tools which we had stowed in our side-bags with the explosives were clearly quite inadequate to break it down or to force the lock. Somewhat dismayed, we rapidly considered placing a charge outside the door. However, on the chance, I thought to try the keys of the house in the Rue Mangeard. The second one turned the lock to perfection and we opened the door. The distributor stood right in front of us, about two metres high with its cables stretching in all directions. We were in some doubt about where to place the charges. Then we noticed that the floorboards were quite loose. We placed one charge right under the distributor and another under the main cables leading from it. We connected three 6-hour time-pencils, intending the charges to go off after midnight. Three was just to make sure that at least one would fire the detonating cord leading to the plastic high explosive.

All this probably took little more than five minutes. We then went out, carefully locking the door behind us. Ascending the steps and entering the courtyard at the back of the Post Office, we recovered our bicycles. Taking a moment to visit a nearby loo we agreed to meet the following morning at a rendezvous close to the Le Mans–Tours road. One or two members of Claude's group would also be there. We separated at the gateway and bicycled off in opposite directions.

When I reached the house which was now our base — the Rue Mangeard was already known to too many people — I had something to eat and then sat on the balcony for a time. It was a fine summer evening and there was a good view of the town. I had hoped to listen for the explosion after midnight, but I found that I could not stay awake. I went to bed and slept peacefully! It turned out that Claude had done the same.

When we met at our rendezvous the following morning we neither of us knew if the charges had gone off. Then one of Claude's group arrived and remarked that the Post Office had been blown up the night before!

It is hard to say how far this episode actually damaged the German communication system. Was the distributor really about to become operative or was it still only in preparation? It was said that it was about to be inaugurated the very next day, and that a German was working on it all that evening — he was apparently having his supper when we made our visit! Most of the telephone lines leading out of Le Mans had been cut anyway.

There was, however, no doubt about the sensation which the action caused both among the citizens of Le Mans and the German forces in the town. That it took place immediately opposite the *Feldkommandantur* certainly made it even more dramatic! In particular it provided a strong boost to the morale of our organization. I had originally hoped to preserve the anonymity of Claude and myself in what we had done. This, however, proved impossible. Claude just had to tell his fellow *résistants*!

There was a barber's shop next to the Post Office and I thought I might get my hair cut there. There was nothing to be seen of the explosion outside, so I went in and the proprietor of the shop duly cut my hair quite uneventfully. As he was finishing the trim I said to him, "There was an incident next door, was there not? "Oh, yes," he said. "Were you affected in any way?" "No, no," he answered me with a smile.

On the Normandy front it was now plain that the Allies were steadily increasing the pressure on the Germans. The break-through could not be far off. On the BBC broadcasts we also heard about the German V1 flying bombs being fired across the Channel. The Allies would certainly be anxious to attack the launching sites as soon as possible.

The Gestapo in Le Mans was obviously seeking to make some arrests following the Post Office affair. I met the proprietor of our former HQ in the Rue Mangeard. She said, vaguely, that there had been some "police enquiries", so they were on our trail! Giving, I hoped, an appearance of total innocence, I renewed the rent, rather to her surprise, and got out of the place as rapidly as I could!

It was shortly afterwards that we heard that our source of information in the Post Office, Monsieur Raguideau senior, had been arrested. Someone must have given him away. He was deported to Germany and did not return.

CHAPTER EIGHT

Ambush

Shortly after the Post Office operation, Claude Hureau's group decided to attack German convoys which were passing through the village of Le Grand-Lucé and "invited" me to participate. Through the news bulletins of the BBC it was evident that the Germans were losing the battle on the Normandy front. It was incumbent on the Resistance to do all we could, no matter how little, to contribute to their discomfiture. For my part, I felt that any reason I had to keep myself free to act as a general organizer and coordinator no longer applied. I said I would gladly join the group in what was to be a major ambush.

The road from Le Grand-Lucé runs over 8 kms to another village, Parigné-l'Evêque in the general direction north-west to Le Mans. About half way was an ideal place to stage the ambush. The road was straight with thick woods on either side and sloping downhill — the better for the German trucks to run off it! There was a minor road running parallel through thick forest which we could use as an approach and, after the attack, retreat through the trees from where we could easily escape on our bicycles.

On the night of 31 July 1944 I joined Claude Hureau, Pierre Raguideau and three other men on the minor road where we were to prepare the attack. We were awaiting three or four more men. I remained with the first three, unpacking our weapons and explosives while Claude and Pierre went off a little way to see where the others might be waiting. Suddenly we heard a pistol shot, then dead silence. Claude and Pierre did not return.

There could be no doubt that we had fallen into a trap. "Arm yourselves" I whispered to the others. Curiously I did not feel fear but only how idiotic we would appear if we were overrun by the Germans with our Sten guns not even assembled. When we were all fully armed I felt much better. Now at least we could put up a fight. Better still though would be to escape!

I felt sure that the Germans would not take long to surround the area in which we had been preparing our ambush. Very reluctantly, I decided that we must abandon our bicycles, with the side-bags stuffed with precious explosives, and make our way through the undergrowth to the main part of the forest.

I led the way, one man looking to the right, another to the left and one to our rear. We made a wide circle around the spot where Claude and Pierre had disappeared — nothing to be seen. Then we came to the minor road along which the Germans must have come. This was the danger point. We braced ourselves and, keeping close together, raced across it. It was a matter of a few seconds. There was no shot! Once in the main forest we were practically safe from pursuit.

Very depressed, we made our different ways to our various safe houses. Of Claude Hureau and Pierre Raguideau we knew nothing. They must be in the hands of the Gestapo. The rest of us would be well advised to look to such security measures as we might be able to take.

Two days later Madeleine returned. All efforts to contact Philippe de Vômecourt had failed. Nor was there any other way of transmitting a message to Buck and the Firm. She brought even worse news. The son of Madame Sevenet — she who had helped us all so much — had been killed fighting in a *maquis* somewhere in Southern France. While staying with Madame Sevenet, Madeleine said, she had been converted to Roman Catholicism.

By this time it did not need the BBC to tell us that the Allies had at last achieved a breakthrough on the Normandy front. German troops in obvious disarray were beginning to stream towards Le Mans from the west along the Laval road. At the entrance to the town stood soldiers of the *Feldgeldarmerie* — in case anyone should mistake them they carried an inscription on a metal plaque across their chests — directing the demoralized men towards the units of the Wehrmacht based in or around Le Mans. They did not interfere with civilians — such as myself for instance!

In fact I recall an incident bicycling along the road to the Château des Bordeaux, with side-bags laden with explosives, when, on a sudden rise over a hill, I encountered a group of German soldiers at the roadside. They took no notice of me and I proceeded on my way, literally slightly hot under the collar.

On 8 August the Germans evacuated Le Mans. The Gestapo took with them about fifty members of Resistance organizations, some of whom must have been captured in the months, or even years, ante-dating my arrival in the Sarthe and others who had been taken prisoner in the Charnie. Philippe and Claude were locked into cells and left behind. They were later released by the French Police. Philippe subsequently confessed that, under torture, it was he who had betrayed the location of the Charnie camp.

That day I went with Madeleine to a meeting with Raimond and a couple of his section leaders. Cycling our way back to Le Mans along the road from Ecommoy we saw two German staff cars pass us. Shortly afterwards one of them came back, travelling at top speed. Thinking little of it we went on for a while and then saw the reason for the Germans' precipitate flight — a column of American troops, including tanks and armoured personnel carriers, was crossing the road in front of us!

At the same time one of our own groups from the area south of Mulsanne had come out into the open amid considerable rejoicing. They had managed to kill one German soldier, presumably whilst trying to escape from the staff car which had been abandoned. I rapidly exerted such authority as I had and requisitioned it. One of the group was a mechanic and quickly rewired the ignition (the Germans had taken the key) and the car started instantly. It was a Steyr painted in

Wehrmacht camouflage colours. Madeleine and I drove off in it with a French flag conspicuously displayed. All the same it was a little disconcerting to have the guns of the American tanks trained on us. We went in search of an officer. We found one and explained our situation to him. He seemed astonished to find English-speaking members of the French Resistance but let us pass without difficulty.

Still in the car, we drove a short way (how much shorter it was by car than by bicycle) to the safe house where Benjamin (RAF) had been concealed for some three weeks. To say that he was pleased that his incarceration was over would be an understatement indeed.

We decided to make our way to Le Mans, only ten to fifteen kilometres away. The Americans would surely be in the town by now. We could hand over Benjamin and establish contact with the American Intelligence HQ, which would now be essential. Consequently, still in our newly acquired Steyr, we took a minor road from a village called Ruaundin. It took us through a stretch of forest. I will admit to a slight feeling of apprehension that the Germans might still be holding out somewhere in the environs of the town. However, Madeleine seemed extremely confident. Benjamin was perfectly content to do what he was told. It seemed a long way to go round the forest by the main roads. Let's just go straight through!

For the first three kilometres the road was deserted. Then, rounding a corner, we saw a detachment of German soldiers barring the way. They seemed somewhat surprised to see a Werhmacht staff car with a tricolour hanging out of the side. I came to a stop and, muttering to Benjamin to stay where he was I got out of the car with Madeleine, calm and attractive as ever. I explained that we had "come by" the car which had been deserted and, taking the attitude that we were devoted collaborators, that we wanted to warn them that the Americans were just down the road. They questioned us for a moment and then the officer who seemed to be in charge suddenly said "Do you speak English?" Was there perhaps a certain "Britishness" about my appearance? As nonchalantly as I could I replied, "*Non, très peu*." He seemed satisfied and after another minute of questioning allowed us to get into the car, turn it round and move off the way we had come.

Once clear, I accelerated rather quickly and wondered if they might take a shot at us. Nothing happened and we turned the corner into the still-deserted piece of road. Suddenly Benjamin, who had fortunately been silent the whole times said reflectively, "Why did those Jerries let us go?" Interesting question!

On the very night, 4 August 1944, that the Americans began encircling Le Mans from west and south, a group connected with our organization ambushed a German convoy, probably endeavouring to escape the rapidly closing trap, at St Mars sur Ballon. We did not know what went wrong; the men were all experienced in that kind of operation. However, the German troops must have reacted with unusual swiftness the group of five were cut off, surrounded and shot on the spot.

During the following day or two the Americans managed to clear the town of the various pockets of German resistance and to establish a provisional HQ. It was the 5th Armoured Division of General Patton's Third Army and we made contact with Major Batey in charge of Intelligence. He was a very amiable person, was rather surprised to hear of our organization and kindly provided us with US Army "C" and "K" rations. By now our groups had all come out into the open. Raimond and George had joined Madeleine and me and a curious moment of what I can only describe as blankness ensued. We had obviously been operating in a state of considerable mental tension and the sudden release to which we had so much looked forward was disappointing rather than exhilarating. George in any case knew what he wanted to do. His father, a Briton domiciled in Paris, where he was in business, had been interned in Drancy by the Germans. He had now been there for four years and George had set his heart on being somehow in the vanguard of the Allies when they finally reached the internment camp. For this he had to wait in Le Mans until the Germans had been driven back at least to the suburbs of Paris.

Just after the American entry to Le Mans, Madeleine had a brief but remarkably unpleasant experience. I have related how we often took our black market meals in cafés and restaurants particularly frequented by Germans, thus implicitly posing as collaborators. In their enthusiasm at their liberation the local inhabitants rounded up all those suspected of collaboration, including Madeleine! As she was herded into a group of real collaborators, being taken off to have their heads shaved — the usual penalty for women thought to have been too friendly with the Germans — she was able to call out to some members of one of our groups who promptly came to her rescue!

Raimond Glaesner's Activities (from his SOE Personal File)

Area: The Forêt de Berce and surroundings. Telephone lines regularly cut. 110 ambushes, 80 vehicles destroyed or damaged, 600 Germans killed or wounded. Four intelligence missions behind enemy lines after the Americans had captured Le Mans.

Claude Hureau's Report

Seventeen sabotages of telephone lines.

Many attacks on German transport and German soldiers killed or wounded.

Participation in the destruction of a German telephone distributor, Place de la République in Le Mans

Three intelligence missions behind enemy lines after the arrival of the American troops.

These activities resulted in great part in the isolation of the German services in Le Mans. Some days, particularly towards the end of the Nazi occupation, the telephone communications were completely cut. On some nights on the main roads leading from Le Mans not a single enemy vehicle was to be seen. Thus, for instance, Claude and his team lay in wait on the road to Angers without a sign of a vehicle.

Particular mention should be made of the extremely valuable assistance provided by M. Raguideau of the PTT in providing us with information which allowed us to attack a number of vital points on the enemy's systems of communication. Special mention must also be made of the farmers and other members of the civilian population of the Sarthe who supported the Resistance in so many ways. These men and women, unlike those of us who were, in effect, soldiers of SOE, were tied to their families, farms and businesses. Consequently they not only risked everything, but, once under suspicion, were sitting targets for arrest by the Gestapo. I must bear witness to their courage and patriotism.

CHAPTER NINE

With the U.S. Third Army

In talking to the Intelligence staff of the U.S. Fifth Division, Major Batey and his senior officer Lt. Col. Powell, it soon became apparent that they were greatly interested in any information which we could bring regarding German troops beyond their own areas of reconnaissance. This gave us an idea. Why should those of us who still felt that we might make some contribution, however small, to the Allied effort, not carry out undercover missions involving penetration behind German lines? The Americans seemed very supportive of such an exercise. Thus it was that, instead of mourning our losses or celebrating such successes as we had achieved during our operations prior to 8 August, we were able to regard ourselves as a kind of special reconnaissance unit for General Patton's Third Army! In all, our original resistance groups were able to accomplish some fifteen of these undercover missions. I am unfortunately unable to record the various experiences of my friends and colleagues on these expeditions into enemy-occupied territory. Three of those in which I participated will serve to give the reader the general feel of this type of operation.

The first of these was to probe the country which lay east of Le Mans and which would be on the flank of the Third Army's advance to the north-east in the direction of Nogent-le-Rotrou and beyond. Obviously General Patton would not care to have any major German forces lurking on his flank while his divisions were turning north towards Chartres and Dreux.

I set out with three young men from one of Raimond's groups. They had a car which had been thoroughly searched for anything which might be incriminating and which I drove. We had a story, something about wanting to visit the granny of one of us who lived near Chartres. We carried of course the usual identity cards. All went well travelling through the country roads and we saw no sign of the Germans. When we reached the neighbourhood of Châteaudun we thought it better to turn back and report to the Americans that so far all was clear. We decided we could take the main road through Vendôme.

Coming up a short rise at the entrance to the town, we were suddenly confronted with a German checkpoint, quite strongly manned. There was no escape here and we stopped. After a perfunctory look at our papers we were told to get out and a couple of soldiers gave the car a thorough search as they took the seats out. I must confess to a sinking feeling. Might there not be a grenade or a bullet or cartridge case which our search team had overlooked? After all the car had been used to carry them to the scene of ambushes on several occasions. However, nothing turned up. I thought what a fool I had been to assume that the Germans had retreated from the area completely. They evidently held Vendôme in some strength.

When the soldiers had finished searching the car the NCO in charge told my three companions to get in the back. He placed one of the soldiers next to me and he himself sat on the wing, machine pistol at the ready. He then directed me to drive to a house which the Germans had made their HQ in the centre of the town. I thought for a moment of trying to shake him off the wing, leaving the others to deal with the man sitting beside me, but decided that this might be too risky. Apart from a good chance of getting shot we would still be in the middle of German-occupied Vendôme.

The NCO then gave us over to an officer who seemed to be in charge. After looking at our papers again, he said in French, "There is something suspicious about your story [visiting Granny!], but we just don't have time to go into that. In the meantime we are requisitioning your car on behalf of the Wehrmacht. You four can go." Concealing my satisfaction at being neither shot nor handed over to the Gestapo, I looked as grumpy as possible and demanded a receipt for the car which he gave me in a businesslike way. Just out of the door I remembered the map of the area which we had brought with us and demanded it with an air of injured innocence! We were now free but in German-occupied territory and without any means of transport. We decided to call on the local gendarmerie. In response to our story that we were on a reconnaissance mission for the U.S. Army (it sounded pretty thin I must admit) they reacted immediately. Within half an hour we found ourselves seated in a police car with two gendarmes in position in front. The Germans seemed to be quite willing to wave us through their checkpoint. In about an hour and a half we reached the outskirts of Le Mans. Shortly afterwards we were informing Major Batey, our friend in the U.S. Third Army, about such observations as we had been able to make. We gathered later that our friends the gendarmes had had some difficulty with the German controls in returning to Vendôme but had successfully made it in the end.

By the third week of August the Germans were in full retreat from the Normandy front. The U.S. Third Army was beginning to close in on what was now called the Falaise Pocket. U.S. Intelligence was particularly interested to know whether the Germans were evacuating men or armour from the Pocket — or both. Our next mission was to try to find out.

I went this time with Madeleine and a young man from one of the Le Mans groups. He drove the car, which was wood-fuelled. On a longish expedition it would be impossible to buy petrol under the prevailing chaotic conditions.

From Le Mans we proceeded by the country roads to Chartres where we had been given a contact, avoiding both Vendôme and Châteaudun. These places were in process of being liberated. It was impossible to know whether the Germans were still there or the Americans had moved in. Our contact in Chartres gave another safe address in Dreux. North of Chartres the road was deserted and we were soon in the town. Our contact was very helpful. He introduced us to a priest who had just come from Evreux. This was actually in the main line of retreat. He was able to inform us that the German troops were streaming back, under cover of twilight or darkness, out of the Falaise Pocket. He did not see any tanks or heavy vehicles. This was just what we had been asked to find out. We thanked the priest and then determined to report back at once to 5th Div. Intelligence.

The *gazogene* car, having been replenished with wood — how our driver had managed it heaven knows — we set out to return via the small country roads. It seemed better to bypass all towns to avoid the risk of encountering retreating Germans or advancing Americans. Our route involved crossing the piece of country known as the Beauce, a spreading plain which is one of the great wheat-growing areas of France. We were about 20 kms out of Dreux and the road, winding among the cornfields, was completely deserted when we were suddenly confronted by a vision of the Apocalypse. On a road which crossed the one we were following was a vast column of men, stretching as far as the eye could see. It was the German Army, in total rout, streaming towards the east. The soldiers were shambling along without any formation or semblance of discipline. There was hardly any transport to be seen, only one broken-down tank, which seemed hardly able to keep its place in the column. Somewhere in the direction of Dreux rose a huge column of black smoke.

It was impossible to contemplate this scene without having to deal with a matter of immediate concern. Somehow we must cross this river of men. There was almost no gap in the flow. On no account must we stop or the least we could expect was that the car would be seized. Finally we discerned a slight break and our driver pressed the accelerator. A few Germans scattered but did not attempt to stop us. In an instant we were through.

We travelled without further incident back to Le Mans where our American friends were considerably interested in what we had to report. The Falaise Pocket was now closing fast and the Allied Armies were moving to the east.

It was obvious that the Germans would not be able to put up any real resistance to the Allied thrust west of Paris. They were withdrawing all their troops from the area of the Loire. We heard on the radio that the Allies had landed in the south of France and seemed to be progressing up the Rhône valley. It was time for George to make his dash to Drancy. He duly left Le Mans in the wake of the French Division under General Leclerc. We did not, of course, know what had become of him. Later we learned that he had succeeded in the plan on which he had set his heart. He managed to arrive at the Drancy camp just after the German guards had left and before the advancing troops of the Allies had arrived. He was able to say that he liberated his father. It was a well-deserved reward for all he had been through.

During the latter part of August the U.S. Third Army was rapidly advancing to the south of Paris. There was very little German resistance here and the Wehrmacht was in full retreat. Some of us continued to carry out reconnaissance missions and to contact local groups of French *résistants* or *maquisards*. Our tasks were made much easier, partly by the disorganized state of the Germans but also by the fact that we had been able to provide ourselves with a variety of documents seized from various collaborators by the new French authorities in Le Mans. These consisted of passes, special identity cards, permits for being out in curfew time and even for carrying weapons! Also available was a man who had acted as interpreter to the *Kommandantur* (we did not ask if he had been a collaborator!) and was able to write in perfect German[1]. Friends in a printing house in Le Mans were able to run off any or all of these papers as required!

So it was that we set out on various expeditions equipped with German documents showing us to be total collaborators with the German occupation. Mine, for instance, carried my photograph duly stamped by the "Security Services", allowing me to circulate by day or night even in forbidden zones and to be armed. The only thing we needed was a pass to allow us re-entry to the ever-shifting lines of the U.S. Third Army. The Lt. Col. in charge of the Counter Intelligence unit (CIC)

---

[1] The interpreter showed us photographs of the senior members of the German Authority of Occupation of the Sarthe. Among them Madeleine and I were able to recognize our dinner-table companion at the Restaurant des Ifs, Herr Jancke, the Chief of the Gestapo for the area!

obligingly signed suitably impressive documents, informing the reader that we must on no account be hindered in the execution of our important duties!

As it turned out the crossing of the, at that time rather fluid, lines between the Armies was surprisingly easy. There was only one danger. If the Germans should thoroughly search us, the discovery of the CIC documents might well prove lethal.

On one occasion Raimond, accompanied by one or two companions, was returning after dark from a visit to a band of *maquisards* somewhere in the vicinity of Orléans. Following the country roads as usual, they lost their way and found themselves confronted by a German guard at some kind of encampment. It was well after the hour of the curfew. The guard immediately became aggressive. While Raimond was turning the car round to try to regain the route they had been following, he demanded to know what they were doing there. Brandishing a pass, in voluble and perfect German, Raimond informed him that the *Geheimestaatpolizei* did not have to account to a miserable soldier for their actions. He finished turning round and drove off at high speed!

General Patton was now driving the Third Army with the Germans before it along an axis Pithiviers, Nemours, Sens, Troyes. It was along the River Seine that the Germans decided to make a stand. In the area of Troyes they had destroyed the bridges and were in positions along the east bank. This brought the Americans to a temporary halt while reinforcements and bridging engineers could be brought up.

Intelligence of 4th Division, the Division immediately facing the Germans across the Seine, was particularly interested to know what, if any, reserves they might be able to call on between the Seine itself and the Marne. At this point the two rivers flow roughly parallel to one another about 70 kms apart. Madeleine and I said that we would endeavour to find out.

On 27 August we set off in a very serviceable Renault car, which we had somehow managed to requisition and plenty of petrol in jerrycans — the American and German containers were almost identical. The first task was to find somewhere where the bridges over the Seine had not been destroyed. Anywhere near Troyes itself was obviously impossible so we drove upstream through a countryside where there had evidently been no military presence, either German or American. On a very small road, just north of Bar-sur-Seine, we found a bridge intact and unguarded. We drove across it and found ourselves in a piece of country apparently untouched by the war. After some 10 kms, passing through a wood, we saw a man at the roadside. I stopped and asked him if there were any *Schleux* (slang for Germans) in the neighbourhood. In a slow drawl he replied, "Well, there were some in 1941." For some distance we drove on uneventfully. Finally we came on a German Army checkpoint. "*Papiere, papiere*," said the NCO in charge. We produced our documents permitting us to travel anywhere, even armed. We passed as a married couple, obviously total collaborators, now fleeing into German-occupied territory for fear of the advancing Americans. The NCO was sympathetic and gave us the go-ahead, but just as I had the car in gear his eye fell on the jerrycans in the back. "German petrol?" he queried. "Yes," I said. Unexpectedly he patted me on the shoulder and we were through.

As we approached the Marne the land was more populated and we were able to approach a number of the local inhabitants. Those who appeared to be friendly and reliable we briefly informed that we were reconnoitring for the Allied advance, which was now imminent. They took us to the banks of the Marne. There seemed to be no sign that the Germans were preparing to make the river a line of defence. There was a story that there might be some German units at Juzennecourt but we were unable to get any confirmation of it. All this took some time and we stayed the night with a friendly farmer and his family.

The next day was fine and we drove along country roads, on our return journey carefully avoiding the checkpoint where we had been held up on the previous day. Everything was peaceful — no sign of Germans or the Americans. After some two hours we were approaching the little bridge over which we had crossed the Seine. It seemed a good moment to hang out the tricolour flag in case the Americans might have moved up the west bank in the last two days.

The road sloped down to the river on a curve and suddenly the bridge came in sight. In front was a group of German soldiers, fully armed. I saw that at least one of them was wearing the black uniform of the SS. The bridge was intact and the road beyond was clear for the short distance that I could see it. I made up my mind on the instant that across the Seine would be either unoccupied country or, better still, the Americans. The car was in third gear. I put my foot down and accelerated and the man guarding the bridge sprang back in astonishment. We were over the bridge and into the approach road when the Germans opened fire. I heard the rear window smash and then, as we ducked as low as we could, I felt a stinging blow in my back, somewhere below my left shoulder. In a moment we were out of sight. On reaching the main road, perhaps 300 metres from the bridge, I had thought to turn right in the direction of Troyes. Impossible — there were more Germans mounting a roadblock. Turning in the other direction towards Bar-sur-Seine, we travelled only a very short distance when we sighted yet another roadblock at the entrance to the town. It was all too clear that we were now completely enclosed by the Germans. We quickly decided to abandon the car. Fortunately the stretch of road where we were was deserted. On the west side was a bank surmounted by bushes. We scrambled up and were glad to get under cover. I could feel the wound in my back but was surprised to find that it did not seem to incapacitate me. There was a small hole in my jacket but very little bleeding underneath. Madeleine had escaped the firing unscathed. After a few moments, as the place still seemed to be deserted, I went back to the car as rapidly as I could and took a bag with our personal belongings out of it and quickly scrambled up the bank again. We decided to go to the west, away from Bar-sur-Seine.

We walked uphill in woodland until we came to a clearing. There was nobody about. There appeared to be a chance we would be able to walk cross-country till we could reach a village or, better still, the American lines. Proceeding a little further we were halted by a German patrol. They made it very clear that on no account would they allow anyone to pass. Apparently they did not connect us with the shooting, which they must have heard an hour or so previously.

There was no way we could get out and decided we would make ourselves less conspicuous by walking into Bar-sur-Seine. The little town was deserted except for German soldiers and their transport. Marked on the latter, I noticed, was a three-pointed star, similar to the emblem of Mercedes-Benz cars. The door of a café was open and we went in. Again the place was deserted. All the inhabitants were sheltering in the cellars. After a little while a number of local men appeared, apparently guarded by Germans, together with a few women. One of the soldiers signed to us that we should join the group. However, after a few minutes, Madeleine was released, together with the other women. She went back to the cafe to collect my coat which I had carelessly left there.

It seemed that the Germans wanted to control our "papers". The prospect did not worry me unduly as I felt my identity card would stand up to even the most rigorous inspection. The American passes were with Madeleine, concealed in a secret pocket in the elastic belt with which SOE's women were provided. After a little while she came back with my coat and told me that she had been able to talk to the fiancée of one of my fellow arrestees who said she could take shelter in the family house. I could come there to pick her up when the Germans had finished checking our "papers".

The time passed. The NCO said that the officer in charge would come "soon". Still no sign of him. It was getting dark as we waited around uncomfortably sitting on benches or on the floor of the café. Gradually the reality of the situation dawned on us — we were hostages against the possibility of the Germans being attacked by the local *résistance*. There was obviously nothing any of us could do. I wondered whether the leaders of any potential attackers were aware of our plight. The hours went by. I lay down on the floor, folded my jacket as a pillow and dozed fitfully. The wound in my back ached.

It was beginning to get light again when an officer came into the café He clearly was in authority and one of my fellow hostages went up to him, declared himself to be the local baker and asked to be released so that he could make some bread. The officer, after a moment's hesitation, agreed to let him go. Thus encouraged, I went forward with my Gestapo-stamped identity card. He took it, went away for a minute or two, handed it back without a word and motioned to me that I could go too. I went out into the square in the centre of Bar. All seemed quiet. Fortunately the local *résistants* had not mounted any kind of attack against the Germans during the night. I was sorry to leave my fellow hostages behind but it was now a question of getting out of the town at all costs.

It was only a little way to the house of the family which had accommodated Madeleine overnight. I duly found it and, very kindly, they insisted on our eating something before what must surely be a long walk. We thanked them for their help and said goodbye. It seemed likely that the Germans would be guarding the west side of the Seine rather than the east. As we were crossing the bridge, still intact, Madeleine said, "Something rather disagreeable happened to me last night."

"What was that", I said.

"When I went to collect your coat in the café there were two German soldiers there and they assaulted and searched me at gun-point." I was speechless. She went on, "Luckily they didn't discover the American passes." What could I say? We went on, gradually leaving the town behind us. At a point where houses ceased altogether we were stopped at a German checkpoint. The NCO carefully inspected our papers. He looked at me, his face full of suspicion, but in the end he let us go. We walked on — free at last from Bar-sur-Seine.

We decided that our best course would be to attempt to join the line of what must surely be the American advance from Troyes. To this end we walked steadily north along totally deserted roads. Our first stop was at a place called Villy-en-Trôde where we thought we might get some information as to the military situation and possibly get some food and rest. We found the village totally deserted. There was no alternative but to go on. This time we thought that the main line of U.S. Third Army advance would be in the direction of

Vendeuvre and Bar-sur-Aube. We continued to walk until we reached the main road from Troyes. No sign of the Americans and again the road was deserted. Eventually we found a farmhouse where we were able to stay overnight. The kind people gave us something to eat. We were surely looking, as we pretended to be, like refugees from one or other of the cities.

Next day we made up our minds to get across the Seine. The Americans were clearly not moving forward from Troyes for the time being. After walking for perhaps a couple of hours along yet another country road we finally came to a bridge over the river. It had been blown up by the retreating Germans who, however, seemed now to have completely abandoned the area. The concrete blocks gave us a rather precarious foothold and we were able to scramble across without too much difficulty. Fortunately the river was quite low. Once across we were quickly able to reach the main road leading along the west bank towards Troyes.

To our joy we saw a US Army jeep travelling along it toward us. We were able to halt the driver and showed him the U.S. Army passes which Madeleine had been so carefully concealing. We then demanded that he should drive us immediately to the Divisional HQ in Troyes. Obviously impressed, the GI told us to get into his jeep. Twenty minutes later we were reporting to the Intelligence Officer of 4th Division.

It must be said that the Americans really showed their appreciation of our efforts. The I.O. escorted us to the office of the General where we passed on as much information as we had been able to obtain, particularly regarding the apparent absence of German preparations for a defence of the line of the Marne. It seemed that a major German unit mainly composed of the 15th Panzer Grenadiers had come up from the south and temporarily occupied Bar-sur-Seine. Their emblem was the Mercedes-Benz three-pointed star. While we were talking the General's assistant produced some substantial Army rations and made us scrambled eggs. It was not long before they were dealt with!

After the conversation with the General I was taken to the medical department and given an x-ray for the wound in my back. The doctor said that some small pieces of metal were lodged just below the shoulder blade. I had been lucky; the bullet must have struck something at the rear of the car. He decided to leave the pieces in. In fact, the wound soon healed over. Some years later, when my back had to be x-rayed for some other reason, they had disappeared!

After a night at a hotel which had been requisitioned by the U.S. Army, Madeleine and I rejoined Raimond and others of our group at our provisional HQ somewhere south east of Troyes.

I must admit to a rather hazy recollection of the events in which I was involved during the first week or two of September 1944, but one incident stands out in my memory.

In visiting a French Resistance organization not far from Chaumont, still on a mission for U.S. Third Army, I was told that they had just captured a German Major who had probably been responsible for the murder of some of their partisans. They said that they were checking this but if he were guilty he would be shot the following morning. I thought that I might be able to obtain some useful information from him and asked the *maquisards* if I might interrogate him. He seemed a pleasant enough man. I didn't know whether he knew how near he might be to possible execution. He turned out to be surprisingly forthcoming. Talking in reasonable French, he gave me the names, numbers and movements of quite a number of German Army units, just what I was looking for of course. At length he suddenly asked, "Is it right that I should be giving you all this information?" I assured him that it was. Yet somehow his confidence in me seemed touchingly pathetic. Madeleine, who was with me at the time, gave him some American chocolate and cigarettes. I do not know whether the *maquisards* executed him or not.

About the middle of September 1944 the Allied armies had liberated nearly all of France. I drove nearly to Nancy from Paris in a day, on a road choked with military convoys to say goodbye to our friends of U.S. Third Army. It was little more than a month since they had entered Le Mans. What a distant past it seemed and how much had happened since the day we had encountered Major Batey and Lt. Col. Powell. At this point I should like to record our appreciation of the help which our reconnaissance parties received from the Americans, particularly in the way of documentation enabling us to return to the Allied lines and in such matters as the provision of petrol supplies and emergency accommodation. We were pleased to have contributed, however little, to General Patton's Third Army in its swift advance through Le Mans to the Marne and beyond.

All the SOE F Section agents who had survived capture by the Gestapo came at this time to Paris. Buck had come over from London. Philippe de Vômecourt joined us and several others who had been operating in different parts of France. I was pleased to see how many of the ex-prisoners of Eysses who had been in the party which crossed the Pyrenees had been recruited into F Section. Like Raimond Glaesner, they had gone through an intensive SOE training and then been parachuted into France to lead and support Resistance groups just about the time of D-Day.

Prominent amongst the F Section agents was Guy d'Artois, Madeleine's husband, who had been a *maquis* leader in the region of Burgundy. The three of us met at what had once been the most famous tearoom in Paris. It can be said that this was probably the most depressing moment in the lives of all three of us. Madeleine did not leave Guy under any illusion as to what her relationship with me had become and yet she was totally determined to make her future life with him.

There was nothing more for any of F Section's agents to do in France and most of us returned to London. I saw Madeleine twice more, once on the flight from Paris and once at a meeting at one of the Firm's houses — 59 Wimpole Street. On the latter occasion she was looking very smart in FANY uniform. The pretty girl, almost a teenager, who had dropped into the Sarthe by parachute in late May was now a beautiful woman. In the summer of 1944 one matured quickly. Raimond was recruited into the new French army. George, who had lost the sight of one eye in his bicycle accident, was demobilized. Buck organized a farewell gathering of all his surviving agents. How many there were who were missing. Some would later return from concentration camps after the war was over but there were many who would not. It was certainly an emotional event.

My wife Joan came from Shrewsbury to London to welcome me back, delighted of course that the whole French campaign was over. I met her at Paddington station and we took a taxi to a hotel near Orchard Court in which the Firm had taken a room for us. On the way I told her that I had been, and still was, in love with someone else. It was now all over. Unsurprisingly, she was tremendously shocked. We spent the next few days in London in a state of complete neurosis.

I was not only depressed but I became aware of a change in my personality. The process had begun on my return from the *Maison Centrale d'Eysses*, but the events of the summer of 1944 had certainly enhanced it. In particular I no longer fitted into the society to which I had been more or less adapted in pre-war days.

CHAPTER TEN

An Assessment

At this point I should like to interrupt my story in order to make some assessment of the French Resistance movement as I was able to see it. Of late there have been quite a number of unpleasant revelations of the extent to which various individuals, particularly some of those occupying positions of authority in the government or in the Civil Service, had actively collaborated with the Germans. To be singled out for their infamy were those who participated in the arrest and the transportation of the Jews to the extermination camps of Hitler's Reich and those who infiltrated the Resistance organizations in order to betray them to the Gestapo. Those organizations based entirely in France or reporting through a headquarters in France to General de Gaulle's office in London were particularly vulnerable to infiltration. There was certainly an element of pride, encouraged by the General himself, in being totally independent of British or US control. He apparently had a particular dislike of F Section SOE which resulted in the latter only being able to recruit French-speaking Britons, not French nationals, for training as its agents. The ex-prisoners of the *Maison*

Centrale d'Eysses were exceptions to this rule. As I have pointed out several times in my account of various events in the Sarthe, the strategy of using watertight units, their headquarters reporting direct to London, rendered the F Section networks much less liable to infiltration than their Gaullist counterparts. As an illustration of the situation, I remember reading of one courageous Frenchman who, on being invited to join one of F Section's networks, said that although he knew that by doing so he would be participating in a more efficient, more secure, and better armed organization, he deemed it a patriotic duty to join a "purely French" (i.e. Gaullist) one.

As the reader will have seen, the brothers Werther and I were obviously denounced to the Vichy Police by some unknown person. Our subsequent interrogation (by Colonel Leprêtre), the trial in Lyons and imprisonment at Eysses were all the work of the collaborationist Vichy authority. I shall not forget, however, how, at the last moment someone saved me from being handed over to the Gestapo, probably on the pretext of my being *accusé* in a Vichy show trial.

From our escape from Eysses, the traverse of the Pyrenees to the entire network in the Sarthe, how many Frenchmen and Frenchwomen risked their lives for what we called *la cause*? There were, it is true, one or two cases of individuals who were captured and, under some form of torture, gave really damaging information to the Gestapo, the most serious being the location of the *maquis* in the forest of the Charnie. It has to be said also that in the months, even years, before our team came to the Château des Bordeaux, the Resistance in the Sarthe had already paid a heavy price in terms of arrests, executions and deportations to the concentration camps of Germany, deportations from which many prisoners did not return. I must, however, bear witness to the fact that our entire organization was only infiltrated once by the "Norwegian", who turned out to be a Gestapo agent.

I feel that there is, or was, a serious problem relating to what one may call the "ethics of resistance". When the whole of Europe was overrun by the German armies it will be remembered that Winston Churchill issued his famous call to set Europe ablaze. SOE was set up with this intention. At that time it seemed that the invasion of Britain was imminent and that anything that would distract the Germans or interfere with their lines of communication could only be to the good. In those days the only ethics involved were manifestly those of self-preservation!

By the summer of 1941 much had changed. The invasion of Britain seemed no longer even a possibility now that the German army was fully occupied in fighting the Soviet Union. In December the Japanese bombed Pearl Harbor and the United States entered the war. Perhaps the ethical aspect of setting Europe ablaze was, at this point, more in doubt. It must have been clear to the Allied leaders, certainly to Churchill, that any possible invasion of the Continent could only be in the distant future. I have briefly described how a typical Resistance organization could evolve through contact with a few friends, in time mushrooming out into uncontrollable ramifications. Sooner or later infiltration or mere gossiping would inevitably alert the Gestapo or the Vichy Police. Thus in the years, say, from 1941 to 1943 the members of many *réseaux*, both SOE and Gaullist, paid a heavy price.

Brian Rafferty was one victim of this premature development of Resistance networks. George Jones, except for his miraculous escape from the Gestapo, would have been another. I was fortunate (although I hardly appreciated it at the time!) by being put in cold storage for fifteen months. In the Sarthe it may be said that it was only a matter of a month or two, if the Americans had not overrun the area, before the Gestapo would have begun to infiltrate our organization with its consequent inevitable destruction.

With the wisdom bestowed by historical hindsight one may think that it would have been better only to encourage the active development of French Resistance networks when there was a real prospect of an eventual D-Day. These would, of course, have to have been exceptions as in the case of specific targets such as armament factories and perhaps the railways. If the Allies had followed such a policy of limitation until, say, the winter of 1943–44, many of those who were in fact shot or deported in the intermediate years would have made an invaluable contribution to operations in the summer of 1944. Many brave men and women had been executed or deported when *Le Jour J* (D-Day) finally arrived.

However, it may well be argued that it was in those intermediate years that the flame of resistance to the

Germans, only flickering in the early months of the Pétain régime, was kept alive and eventually fanned into the blaze which Churchill had envisaged. It certainly must have been worrying for the German authorities of occupation that the mass of the French population was at least passively and often actively against them.

In a historian's view of the hierarchy of evil which constituted Hitler's Third Reich, pride of place could well be given to the Gestapo, the German Secret State Police. This organization was responsible for the systematic persecution and extermination of the Jews and for the deportation and the death of thousands of men and women of other faiths or of none in the concentration camps.

A distinction should perhaps be drawn between the part played by the Gestapo in perpetrating its innumerable crimes against innocent human beings and its role in defending the Wehrmacht from guerrilla warfare and sabotage along the lines of communication to the front. This was indeed a type of warfare which knew no rules. Men in civilian clothes would attack military convoys, women would carry clandestine messages, railways and telephone lines would be blown up, partisans would hide up in farms and town houses. This was total war. Those of us who participated in it knew the price which might have to be paid.

I mentioned earlier that I was conscious of a change in my own personality. This was probably the case of many men and women over the war years and nowhere more than in the SOE. The actual changes might be different from person to person but events would make their mark. As for me, I think I could say that I was both tougher and yet more idealistic — a curious combination.

As far as toughness is concerned the following story may illustrate the kind of shift of attitude which the preceding two years had wrought in me. In some area bordering on the Sarthe an independent Resistance group had come to the conclusion that a local girl had been gossiping about their activities and that the gossip had reached the ears of the Gestapo. Knowing where she lived some of the group had gone to the house at night, seized the girl, stripped her naked, tied her to a lamp post in the village square, painted a swastika on her forehead and hung a placard round her neck on which was inscribed "*ma langue etait trop longue*" (my tongue was too long). At the time I had thought this almost a joke and that it served the girl right. It was only when I recounted this incident to some British friends, on my post-France period of leave, that, seeing the incredulous revulsion on their faces, I began to realize that my outlook on life had hardened.

So much for toughness. What about idealism? I now had a strong feeling that our pre-war society must be radically changed. The class distinctions, the lack of opportunity for some of the more able, the inequalities of wealth and the poverty of the disadvantaged could no longer be tolerated by the men and women who had been so determinedly engaged in the struggle against Germany and Japan. At the end of the First World War they had said that Britain would be a land fit for heroes. We all knew what had become of that boast. It would be, must be, different this time. I bought a book of Stalin's writings and speeches and, slightly tongue in cheek, declared myself to be a Communist. It will be recalled that in those days, Stalin, Uncle Joe as we called him, was our great ally in the war against Hitler. The Soviet Union was perhaps the land of a new kind of society, with Karl Marx as its prophet. One thing was very evident; in spite of its losses in manpower and territory, the Soviet Union was now driving the Germans back on all fronts. That good old Uncle Joe was actually Hitler's rival in brutality and murderous cruelty was totally hidden from our eyes. Whatever my illusions about Communism, I was certainly not alone in thinking that after the war a better society must emerge than the one which had gone before.

Most of all I needed a new purpose in life. The Firm seemed to offer a way out. My first idea was to parachute into Germany, appearing as a French prisoner of war who had been forcibly retained in Germany and put to work on a farm or a factory. There were many such persons and, of course, I could easily be provided with the necessary papers — perhaps my pass which had been so useful when crossing the lines in France could be used again. Then, if I could be dropped near a prisoner-of-war camp, perhaps I could contact the inmates with a view to organizing a break-out. Then, if arms could be parachuted in, we could establish small sabotage groups. With this idea in mind, I was introduced to an SOE officer whose responsibilities included infiltrating agents into Germany. He was named Herman and nicknamed Herman the German. In spite of his nickname it soon appeared that any dropping of agents, let alone arms, was totally impossible in the current state of the war.

While I was recovering from the disappointment of, as I now saw it, my quite absurd idea, the Firm came to the rescue and offered me three possible courses. The first was to be demobbed altogether — not to be thought of in my present state of mind. The second was to return to the Royal Fusiliers. Again I knew I would be repelled by the attitudes, rank-consciousness and discipline of regimental life. The third course was to continue in SOE and to move to the Far East — Force 136 as it was called. This would involve parachuting, sabotage and the linking up with partisan bands of local people. This third course was far more to my taste than the other two and I enthusiastically accepted it.

I then went on two or three week's leave. I was more than ever conscious of living in another world. My very attractive wife and my daughter, a pretty little thing now aged two, just did not seem to belong to me. I dutifully visited friends and relations. I was glad when my leave was over. I would now go into a new career. It promised to be quite exciting and venturesome.

I have often thought that the impulse to take risks may be an addiction. Could it be something to do with the adrenalin in one's bloodstream? The first reaction may be fear and then thrill. Climbing on a narrow ridge with a drop of 1000 metres on either side is one example. Parachuting blind into enemy-occupied territory is another; there are many more. I submit that this amounts to a true addiction, maybe based on a physical or psychological cause or, more likely, a combination of the two. It is, of course, not hard to see an evolutionary benefit in this phenomenon. Primitive men as hunters on the savannah might feel fear — a reaction of caution — on approaching a lion and a thrill — a stimulus to action. If the hunter were a bad hunter the lion would be likely to have him for lunch. If he were a good hunter he would return triumphantly to his tribe with the skin of the lion. It would certainly be in the interests of the tribe that he should do it again and again and again. The course of evolution would then favour those hunters who would successfully go after lions with the "fear-thrill" impulse. In succeeding generations they would become genetically inherited! How's that for a piece of amateur psycho-anthropology?

My wife came to see me off at Euston station. An emotional gap now yawned between us but there was nothing to be done. Euston was grey in the late autumn afternoon — everything seemed grey. Suddenly a curious reflection entered my mind. "Where I am going there will be colour." I thought. Then I picked up my bag, said goodbye and entered the train. A moment later it pulled out of the station and chuffed its way through the grey countryside.

CHAPTER ELEVEN

India and Thailand

The SOE "bods" (in the Forces' slang) who had volunteered for service in the Far East were, generally speaking, from two sources. Much the smaller group, of which I was one, was composed of members of the former F Section (Buckmaster) who had served in France as aides to the Resistance, working under cover as part of the civilian population. The larger group was composed of "Jeds". These were men who had taken part in "Operation Jedburgh". This was a major operation which consisted of Frenchmen, Britons and Americans grouped in teams of three. The Brits and the Americans were required to speak some French without, however, being necessarily bilingual. The teams were recruited from the three armies and given special training in guerrilla warfare and sabotage. The Jeds were kept in reserve until D-Day. They were then parachuted, in uniform, to provide support and military expertise to many of the larger *maquis* — those mostly operating in areas of hills and forests which also allowed for large-scale drops of weapons, material and explosives. These *maquis* then openly attacked whatever Germans there might be in their respective areas. It was, incidentally, just such a *maquis* which it had been our ill-fated intention to establish in the Forêt de Charnie.

Although the F Section members and the Jeds seemed to view each other with some reserve in the first stages of our association, it was not long before the differences in our backgrounds were forgotten. As it happened all the bods were quartered in a vast country house which had been home to the Jeds before their departure to the field; a bleak place it was too. However, it was not long before we left by train for Liverpool where we embarked on the good ship *Otranto*. For some reason, no-one was supposed to know that it was the *Otranto* but everyone did! It would have been more appropriately named the "Sardine Tin". It contained, I believe, around 5000 men. Officers such as our group were accommodated in staterooms, magnificently designed for pukkah Sahibs in pre-war days, now housing 26 of us! All the other saloons, dining rooms, etc. were stretched to the limit or, more precisely, the assorted bods were subjected to the limit of squeezing! The November weather made it virtually impossible to go on deck. It was rumoured that our destination would be Bombay.

We stayed in the port of Liverpool for two days and on the third night we were off. Going on deck the next morning and hoping that the voyage during the night would have brought us some way to the south we actually found ourselves anchored in the River Clyde! Another three days went by. I learnt to shave with salt water. I read *Thus spake Zarathustra*, the Koran and of course the works of that great guru Joseph Stalin!

At last the convoy was ready; it must have been composed of some dozen ships. We proceeded down the coast of Ireland and around Spain. After we had been going for about three days I came upon deck early one morning and was suddenly in a transformed world, a cloudless sky and blue sea stretching to the horizon. Perhaps there was hope in life once more.

It was on the *Otranto* that I acquired the name "Soapy" by which I was henceforth known throughout my career in the Far East. In fact all Hudson's soap, of course, a product long since disappeared.

It took us about three weeks to get to Bombay. As we were approaching the port all the troops were issued with sunhelmets. No matter that the need for these had been replaced by a ration of salt tablets and a simple beret — it was the regulation to issue them but not to wear them! After putting them on for a few minutes and saying to each other, "Dr. Livingstone, I presume," we decided to leave them on the ship, dedicating them to bureaucracy.

Bombay was a revelation of poverty and dirt, contrasting extremely unpleasantly with the *Herrenvolk* attitude of the British rulers of India. I walked from the port into the city with three friends from the *Otranto*. Two of these were female doctors and one a male Jed. We were appalled at the crowds of beggars, men, women and children, many of them with some piteous disability.

Somehow or other we managed to end up at the Bombay Officers' Club. Here was another shock. On the well-kept lawn a uniformed band was playing. The well-groomed officers and other Sahibs, also some "mems" (memsahibs), sat around drinking their gin and tonics in the evening light before going into their dinner in the palatial colonial building. Did no-one tell them there was a war going on? Memories of Eysses and Le Mans came back to me. Then there was the vision of the beggars we had just encountered, and what about my egalitarian philosophy? "Let's get out of here," I said, and my friends were entirely in agreement. I should add that my repulsion at the atmosphere of the Officers' Club was entirely due to philosophic considerations and not — repeat not — to the particularly snobbish notice on the wall of the bar to the effect that, although the Club would accept the presence of Captains and subalterns, only officers with the rank of Major and above were permitted to buy drinks. As it happened, I had been promoted to Major and my three friends were all Captains!

Anyway, we turned away from the whole gathering and, after eating a modest meal in a restaurant, we went back to the ship.

Our whole SOE group was transferred to a camp outside Bombay and shortly afterwards embarked on a train journey across Southern India. Our destination was Ceylon (now Sri Lanka). The proceedings were uneventful except for a particularly interesting conversation I had one evening with an Indian lawyer, also on his way to Ceylon. The evidence of class and caste distinctions, I said, I found totally repellent and it did not surprise me that Gandhi and Nehru were trying to raise a revolution against the British Raj. He astonished me by saying, "It's really you British who have introduced these ideas of social justice and equality." "Surely the British have done their best to create a kind of master-race mentality," I countered. "Yes," he said "in India, but it is those Indians who have been educated or trained in Britain or exposed to the British way of life who have returned to India with a new vision of society. India has for hundreds of years accepted a caste system. The British added just one more caste. They have also provided us with quite a good administration. But eventually, of course, they will have to go!" he added with a pleasant smile.

Ceylon was an extraordinary contrast to India. The lush green forests, plantations and paddy fields made us look forward to being established there for a time. Our camp was about thirty miles from Colombo at a place called Horana. This was where we were to be trained in jungle warfare preparatory to being dropped into one of the countries occupied by the Japanese. This included Burma, from only part of which the 14th Army under General Slim had managed to drive out the Japanese forces after much bitter fighting. SOE's task would be to inspire and mobilize the peoples of South East Asia: Burmese, Thais, Malays, Laotians and Vietnamese and generally to make life as unpleasant as possible along the Japanese Army's lines of communication. More especially it would be along these lines that the Japanese would be forced to retreat from Burma. 14th

Army's offensives which were now gathering strength by the day could be expected to clear the whole country back to the Thai border by, maybe, the autumn of 1945.

The Horana camp, it was said, had been located by a senior SOE officer, more enthusiastic than knowledgeable, in what he believed to be a forested jungle ideal for training. There was only one snag. The "forest" consisted of plantations of carefully tended trees without any undergrowth at all! The nearest real jungle was thirty miles away. Nonetheless we settled in to comfortable huts, ate well and attended lectures on warfare in South-East Asia.

At the Horana camp the bods of F Section and the Jeds were joined by a number of "Chindits". The Chindits were the creation of General Orde Wingate, a strange and powerful personality, who had been killed in an aeroplane crash on 24 March 1944. His great accomplishment and that of his Chindits had been to show that British troops combined with Indians and Gurkhas could match the Japanese in jungle warfare. Not only that. They succeeded in operating far behind the enemy lines supplied by parachute drops, cutting communications and generally creating havoc in the rear of the Japanese army. To carry out these operations, the Chindits were subjected to very intensive training in survival techniques as well as guerrilla tactics. Wingate inspired his men with a willingness to fight the Japanese on what had hitherto been regarded as their own ground — the jungles of South-East Asia.

It has to be said that at first the addition of the Chindits to what was called Force 136 aroused, shall I say, a certain amount of antagonism. Wingate's leadership and their major contribution to the Allied campaign in Burma had given the Chindits a certain sense of their own importance. On the other hand, our collective exploits in France had ensured that we had no inferiority complex either! It was, fortunately, not long before the camaraderie of training and living together cured us of whatever doubts we may have had about each other.

There was, however, a serious side to the difference between the Chindits and the ex-France members of Force 136. This was a difference of strategy in behind-the-line warfare. This was, curiously, the difference of approach between two men — T.E. Lawrence (of Arabia) and Orde Wingate himself. They were, in fact, distantly related. Lawrence was, of course, killed in a motorcycle accident some time before the outbreak of the Second World War. Wingate had, at first, admired Lawrence but had later regarded the latter's strategy as flawed and, needless to say, felt that he had devised a much better one.

I may, perhaps, summarize the two apparently conflicting views of the way in which warfare behind enemy lines could be conducted as follows: first, the set-Europe-on-fire approach. Agents would be infiltrated, one way or another, to make use of the population of a country occupied by the enemy. Building on latent or overt resentment to the occupying troops, the locals would be recruited into a coherent organization, trained and armed. The agent, or agents, would contribute the essential leadership and expertise. The groups would live off the country. The Chindit approach, by contrast, involved the locals only to a limited degree. The principal element of what would become guerrilla attacks to break the enemy's lines of communication or sabotaging supplies would be provided by specially trained airborne soldiers supplied by parachute drops, not only with ammunition and explosives, but also with food.

On reflection, it soon became clear that in Force 136 we needed a combination of these strategies according to the various problems which would certainly be facing us when we got into the field.

As part of my training, not long after reaching Horana I was despatched to an area of real jungle in the company of a Chindit major and a group of soldiers also under training. On the first day we "went for a walk" in the jungle. I quickly learnt two things. First, when walking behind someone in thick bush, either follow closely behind the man in front or keep your distance. Both will avoid your getting continuously slapped in the face by bushes! Secondly, in really thick undergrowth where it is impossible to see the horizon you must go by a compass. If not, you are more than likely to find yourself walking in a circle!

We got back that evening to the little camp which we had been allocated for our special jungle experience to find a message waiting for the Chindit major. He was to report immediately to HQ, with unspecified duties. Informing me that I was to replace him for the training of the NCOs and men in jungle warfare, he bade me a cheerful farewell. Undaunted, I thought of the techniques which Raimond and my other friends had successfully used to ambush the Germans in the Sarthe. These would do nicely! We assiduously practised ambushing in the jungle for a week and then returned to Horana.

Apart from the British officers in the camp, there were also a number of individuals from the countries of South-East Asia who were, or who it was thought might be, leaders of resistance to the Japanese occupation. Among those was a Thai officer with whom I became very friendly. I should say that my egalitarian socio-political views did not prejudice me against His Highness Prince Svasti, Lieut. Colonel in Force 136 and generally known as "Chin"! I had always been fascinated by Buddhism and of course Thailand (then known as Siam) was a centre of Buddhist culture. Chin was more than willing to tell me about Thailand and to discuss Buddhism. We used to walk up a little hill near the camp in the evening and look out over the plantations stretching as far as the eye could see — just the place for philosophic contemplation. I vaguely remember drawing a comparison between the teaching of Gotama and that of Epictetus. Both were inculcating a doctrine of non-attachment to material things or to the results of action. Not that one should be inactive in life. Epictetus had said, "If evil men appear thou wilt clear the earth of them." Relevant also to our arguments were the words of Shri Krishna in the Bhagavad Gita; "Nothing can be more welcome to a soldier than a righteous war." "Look upon pleasure and pain, victory and defeat with an equal eye. Make ready for the battle." Nothing said about loving one's enemies!

Chin gave me a good deal of extremely interesting information with regard to the situation in Thailand under the Japanese occupation. The Thais were apparently at one in their dislike of the Japanese. When the Armies of Nippon had invaded and rapidly overrun the whole of South-East Asia, culminating in the capitulation of Singapore, the Thai Government had had at its head an Army General, Marshal Pibul Songgram. Pibul was favourable to the Japanese and was, evidently, something of a collaborator. As the resistance of the Allies hardened and the tide of the war began slowly to turn, a coup took place in Bangkok. It was, it seems, bloodless — apparently all coups in Thailand were bloodless. The result was that the new Prime Minister, Luang Pradit (the King had been exiled in the 1930s) resolved to turn the country in the Allies favour, a dangerous tactic seeing that Japan controlled the whole surrounding area. A first step had been to establish regular contact with the Headquarters of the Allied South-East Asia Command. Somehow, I believe by submarine, a British officer had been smuggled into Bangkok together with a Thai national as his radio operator to assure the liaison. The officer was Brigadier Jacques. In pre-war days Jacques had been a lawyer in Bangkok and spoke Thai fluently. His presence in the very seat of the Thai Government was a marvellously kept secret.

A Thai Section had been set up in the Calcutta HQ of Force 136 with Lieut. Colonel Poynton and Major Gilchrist in charge and a number of agents had been recruited. They were mainly students who had been studying at Universities or technical colleges in the UK. A few, like my friend Chin, were members of the Thai Royal Family. These had been living in Britain since King Prajadhipok had been deposed and exiled in 1933. All were willing to enter Thailand by parachute or landing craft to assist in getting rid of the hated Japanese. The Japanese were particularly detested because Thailand, unlike the rest of South-East Asia, had always been an independent nation, never subject to colonial rule. The Government, it was true, had employed a number of Europeans and Americans, but only in an advisory capacity. Thailand, as the country came to be called in post-war years, was literally translated from Muang Thai — the land, or city, of the free.

In early 1945 only a few Thai agents from Force 136 had been infiltrated. The only Europeans in Thailand were Brigadier Jacques, tucked away in Bangkok, and an American missionary resident in the north-east of the country. Some expertise in the organization and tactics of guerrilla warfare was obviously needed. My colleagues, ex-France and ex-Chindits, all seemed destined for Burma. In a meeting with Colonel Musgrave, the Commandant of the Horana camp, I suggested I might be just the man to help organize resistance in Thailand. Colonel Musgrave communicated this suggestion to the HQ of the Thai

Section of Force 136 in Calcutta. It was graciously approved. Henceforth Thailand was to be my destination.

Having decided that my future area of operations would be Thailand, while I was waiting for something to happen I thought it might be an advantage to acquire the rudiments of the Thai language. During my evening meetings with Chin I started writing down lists of words. In one way it is surprisingly easy, so one thinks, to learn Thai because the actual words are monosyllables. The difficulty arises when one finds out that each monosyllable can carry up to five tones, and the meaning of a word depends on the tone. I am pretty nearly tone-deaf but pursued my linguistic studies as best I could none the less.

I had a short period of leave in the hills of Sri Lanka at Nuwara Eliya and then travelled by warship from Trincomalee to Calcutta. Sleeping on deck under the stars was a glorious feeling until one was abruptly awakened at 6 a.m. by the jolly sailors sluicing down the decks. I spent only a short time in Calcutta before being sent back by air to the Horana camp. Apparently the RAF was not ready to parachute anybody into Thailand.

After a week the order came again to go to Calcutta, this time by train. Chin and a cousin of his made up the party. The cousin, also a prince of course, was a remarkable young man. He had been sent to Europe to gain practical experience in automotive engineering. With this aim he had been apprenticed to a garage in

Marseilles. There he had acquired the French language spoken with the most perfect Marseilles accent that can be imagined! We had been ordered to report to the Grand Hotel, Calcutta, rather suitable accommodation we thought for such worthy characters as ourselves. Well, it was certainly a fine room into which we were shown. It was just too bad that we had to share it with six other officers!

Calcutta was a shock; the poverty and dirt seemed worse than in Bombay. The Officers' Club was at least not so ostentatious. We were soon moved out of the Grand Hotel and I was able to take up quarters with a true-blue British gentleman who must have been a resident of Calcutta long before the war. He had certainly maintained his life-style. He had a staff of eighteen servants and expressed surprise that I had not brought a batman with me. We had the most beautiful mangoes for breakfast, specially brought from Bombay — in the war!

The snobbery of the resident white population of Calcutta was unbelievable. One example: the Tollegunge Club was restricted to members who were not in "trade". It so happened that one man who was in shipping and was a long-standing member of the Club went back to the UK. He returned to Calcutta as the General Manager of the Army and Navy Stores, a huge emporium, certainly the biggest department store in the city. It was generally considered a fine job. Sadly the General Manager had to be asked to resign from the Tollegunge Club — he was now in "trade".

Still no possibility of dropping into Thailand. I was given ten days' leave and went up to Darjeeling, a wonderful climate after Calcutta, one glorious view of Kanchenjunga, but otherwise a remarkably dull place. I went on a trek and was disappointed to find that there was no chance of seeing the Himalayas. It was just a matter of walking along deep valleys among the foothills.

I returned to the humid heat of Calcutta. VE day passed almost unnoticed. The war against Germany had already seemed a foregone conclusion. I accompanied Chin on a training parachute drop. Before embarking on a new expedition into enemy occupied territory we were asked if we would care to carry an "L tablet" in a convenient uniform pocket. "L" stood for lethal and the "tablet" consisted of potassium cyanide. I had refused this offer in my days with the French Resistance, feeling that if I were ever arrested by the Gestapo I might have a chance of bluffing my way out of the situation. If I were to be searched, the discovery of an "L tablet" would be just about the end of any bluff. If I were to be caught by the Japanese, however, there would be no chance for any bluff and from what one had heard about the Kempetai — the Japanese counter-intelligence organization — they would certainly not refrain from torture. Nevertheless, I declined the L tablet and opted in favour of a tube of morphine tablets. A more comfortable end, I thought. I was assured that if I swallowed the lot no one would be able to do anything about it.

Finally, towards the latter part of May '45, the order came to go to Jessore. There was a large airfield and it was from this airfield that many flights had taken off carrying men and supplies in furtherance of behind-the-lines activities. I was given a companion — yet another Thai prince, even more senior than Chin. Nicky was the name we knew him by and he was a pilot Flight Lieutenant in the RAF. Our mission was to liaise with the Thai Force 136 agents who had been dropped into north-east Thailand a couple of months previously. Then, working with them, to reconnoitre possible airstrips where Dakotas or similar supply-carrying aircraft could land. This task was complicated by the onset of the rainy season which would render potential runways dangerous by causing them to become waterlogged. This was where Nicky was to come in. The RAF would not trust anyone who was non-RAF with the assessment of any airstrip on which their planes might land.

At the last moment I was invited to a hasty session with a photographic expert. I learnt "all about photography" in about an hour; starting from scratch! Then I was entrusted with a beautiful Leica-type camera with the suggestion that it might be useful to take photographs of any airstrips or dropping grounds as part of our reconnaissance.

We took off from Jessore at night in a four-engined bomber and by the time dawn broke we were well clear of the Burma-Thailand border. We flew on for perhaps an hour. Then the dispatcher connected our parachutes and we felt the plane circle. He took the cover off the hole in the floor and we saw we were passing over thick forest. Suddenly there came a clearing.

The dispatcher shouted "Go". Then the familiar steeling of the nerves, the drop, the buffeting of the slip-stream, the jerk of the 'chute opening and the sensation of floating down. I could see we were in a large open space with quite a few people around. I landed easily enough and, as my parachute training demanded, immediately began to fold up my 'chute. A rather thickset Thai man of about 30 years of age in British tropical uniform and wearing a Captain's shoulder badges, came up to me. In excellent English he said, "Never mind about that. Let's get off the ground quick." He escorted me, also Nicky who had landed nearby, to a large hut made of bamboo. "It was better to get you off the ground," he explained. "There were quite a few locals watching and there aren't many European faces around these days!"

Our new friend (his name was Snoh Nilkamhaeng and his code name Chew) proceeded, over a pleasant meal, to give Nicky and me a general view of the situation in north-east Thailand, something of which we had only vaguely been made aware before our departure from Calcutta. We were actually now the guests of the Royal Thai Air Force at an airfield about 90 kms east of a town called Khonkaen. Chew and his radio-operator, code named Noon, had been dropped about three months previously and set up their base there. The RTA itself was a remarkably active body. Anti-Japanese to a man, they possessed in our area perhaps ten planes. These were truly vintage specimens, all biplanes dating from the twenties with air-cooled engines. Marvellously, and with what must have been a total absence of spare parts, the Thais had succeeded in making these antiques serviceable and indeed they were to be our sole means of transport within Thailand during the ensuing months. The Japanese, totally occupied by the ferocious battles in Burma, had left the whole of northern Thailand devoid of troops or even any authority of occupation. It seemed that there would be plenty of scope for Force 136 to prepare some kind of organization which could operate in the rear of the Japanese army when it would, in all probability, be forced back from Burma into Thailand. Chew already had the RTA committed to assist in any operation which we might plan.

The immediate task for Nicky and me was to discover which of the several airstrips in the area might be the most suitable for landing Dakotas. The one we had actually parachuted on from the plane which had brought us from Jessore was at a place called Khonsan about 90 kms west of Khonkaen. This was judged as likely to become too soft if there was much rain. There were several other possibilities. We flew to each of them and finally we, or rather Nicky, settled on Naarn close to the little town of Loei. The area was remote from anywhere the Japanese might be. It was in hilly country not far from the border with Laos.

In the meantime, with the help of the Thai Air Force, I did a bit of reconnoitring of possible dropping grounds. There was one superb place — a tabletop mountain over 1500 metres high with forests

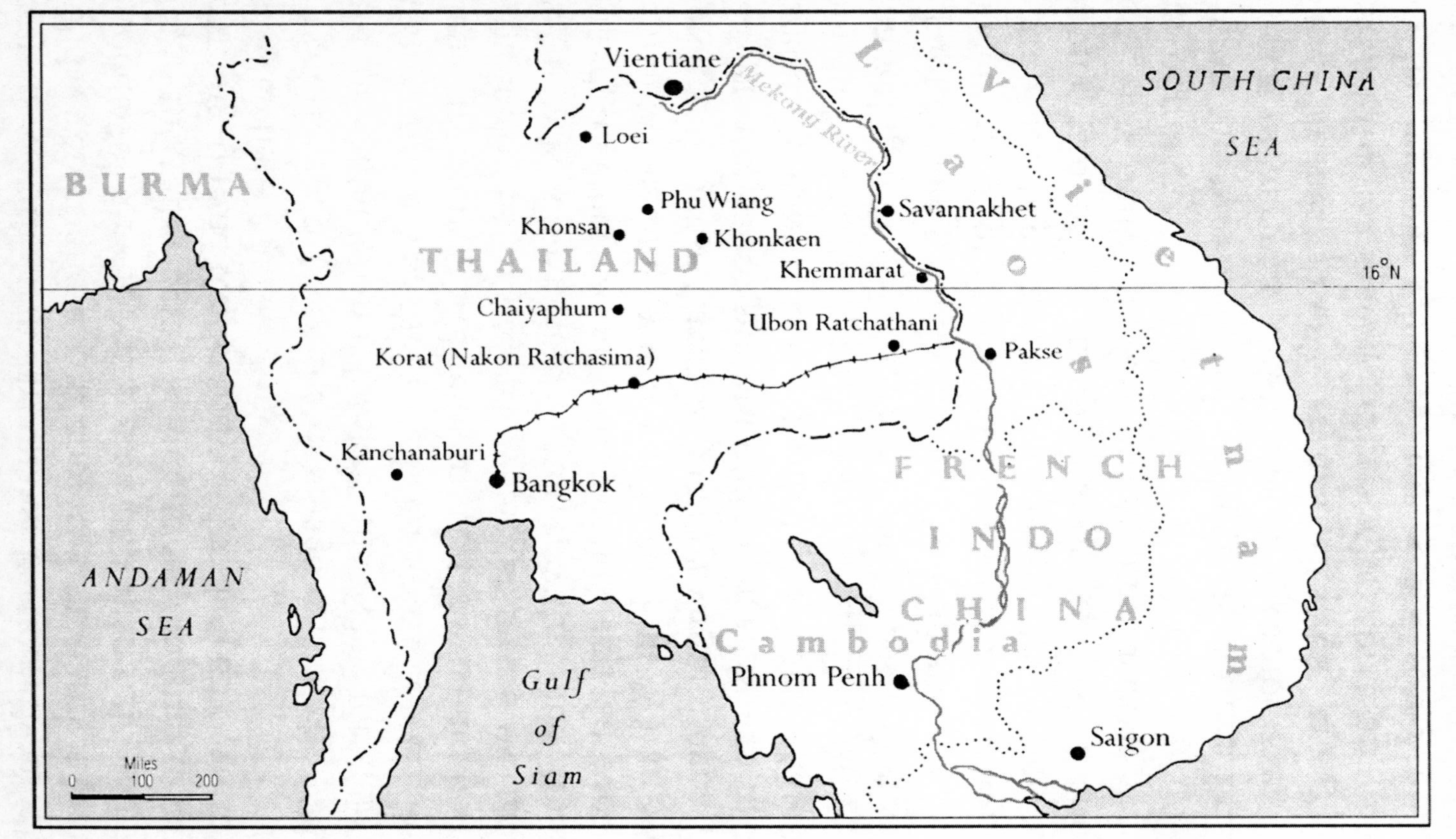
BURMA
THAILAND
Laos
Vietnam
FRENCH INDO CHINA
Cambodia
SOUTH CHINA SEA
ANDAMAN SEA
Gulf of Siam
Vientiane
Mekong River
Loei
Phu Wiang
Khonsan
Khonkaen
Savannakhet
Khemmarat
16°N
Chaiyaphum
Ubon Ratchathani
Pakse
Korat (Nakon Ratchasima)
Kanchanaburi
Bangkok
Phnom Penh
Saigon
Miles
0
100
200

interspersed with open savannahs. Particularly nice for a holiday resort and a golf course, I thought! It would be wonderful for dropping men and materials, but the route to the valley below would be far too long to carry everything down. Reluctantly I decided that we must look elsewhere.

From the map I saw that a village called Phu Wiang might be suitable and I asked the RTA for help in enabling me to see the area from above. As the little biplane circled over it, I felt sure that this would be just the place for us to prepare whatever forces we might have. It was almost like a crater with a few houses grouped together, some paddy fields and an area of savannah. The hills which encircled Phu Wiang were covered with dense forest, apparently virgin jungle. The place was only accessible through a narrow gap in the hills and the approach was limited to a track which led about 40 kms north from the Khonkaen-Khonsan road. By shouting and gesticulating I somehow indicated to the pilot that he should take the plane on another circle and leaning out of the open observer's seat, pointed the camera I had been given in Calcutta at the prospective dropping ground. I snapped away as best I could, feeling very doubtful whether anything useable would come out of it.

About this time the Thais brought us in three British prisoners of war who had managed to escape from one of the Japanese POW camps situated along the Thailand-Burma railway. There were not many such. They had actually effected their escape some months previously and had been hidden and cared for by the

Thais. They were certainly in much better condition when they were handed over to us than they must have been in the camp. They had absolutely harrowing stories to tell about the privations suffered by the men who had laboured on the railway. To the Japanese, soldiers who surrendered were objects of contempt, deserving only to be exploited. The three British escapers were also supremely conscious of having been members of the garrison of Singapore. They viewed the surrender as shameful. I had to reassure them that no-one in the UK would dream of holding them personally to blame for this humiliating chapter of the war.

After a week we had completed our reconnaissance and Nicky and I were ready to return to Calcutta and report. We sent a message via Noon that we would await a plane to pick us up at Naarn. Sure enough within a couple of days a Dakota duly arrived, circled, saw our signals and landed without a hitch. We anticipated that the Captain and his crew might be feeling a little nervous at landing on this somewhat primitive airstrip hundreds of miles behind the Japanese lines. Putting on his RAF peaked cap and displaying his Flt. Lt. shoulder badges, Nicky boarded the plane as soon as the door was opened and reassured everyone that they could safely come out and that refreshments were waiting at the side of the strip. The pilot could then inspect it at leisure. Everyone relaxed; the strip was judged to be satisfactory. Nicky and I and the three ex-POWs got in and the crew readied the plane for take-off. We need not have worried about the state of the ground or the surrounding forest. We were only about halfway down the strip when the marvellous Dakota seemed to spring into the air. By the time we came to the trees they were far below.

The flight was without incident. The pilot carefully avoided the large thunderclouds which accompany the monsoon and we touched down, I think, at an airfield somewhere in the Arakan. Our ex-prisoners were amazed to see the rows of fighter planes waiting on the tarmac; they almost wept. After refuelling we flew on to Jessore and by the usual hot road to Calcutta.

We were able to give HQ quite a good report on the situation in the Khonkaen-Loei region and I was enthusiastic regarding the possibilities of a very substantial build-up of men and materials in the hills and forests. I was able to affirm that the Thais, as far as I could see, would be totally in support of the Allied campaign. It would be easy to live off the land; rice was grown everywhere. Then I took my camera and the exposed film back to the service photographer. It was rather exciting to see what would come out when he developed it. First of all nothing happened, just the background of the jungle. "No good," I said, disappointed that I had not done better. Suddenly there appeared a light patch in the extreme corner of one photograph. Then, with considerable skill, the expert brought the light patch into the middle of the picture and then enlarged it by several degrees of magnification. Finally, as he drew the photograph from the developing bath, a perfect aerial picture appeared of the Phu Wiang dropping-ground. We congratulated each other. Obviously this would prove enormously useful to the pilot of any plane preparing to drop men or supplies.

I found that the RAF could not land me back in Thailand for at least a couple of weeks. I stayed in Jessore, hot, bored and impatient! There were only two paperbacks to read, one a history of the ancient Britons, the other a book of Indian pornography, the one as dull as the other in my then state of mind!

Towards the middle of June the RAF was ready for me. In the meantime quite a few things had happened. The Japanese were being steadily pushed back in Burma. Rangoon had been captured and the 14th Army was being steadily reinforced now that the war in Europe had come to an end. An American officer had been landed at an airstrip about 20 kms from Khonsan. (Nicky had regarded that airstrip with disfavour, but the Americans had seemed to have been able to use it.) A British officer had been dropped in the area of Sakhon Nakhon — Major David Smiley, ex-SOE Albania. He had, however, met with a nasty accident. One of the Firm's patent briefcases, designed to explode should an unauthorized person tamper with it, had gone off unexpectedly and burnt David's arm quite badly. It was evident that he would have to be evacuated from the field to receive medical treatment. The Thai Air Force took him to Naarn so that the RAF could pick him up.

I had now been allocated an NCO specialist weapons instructor and together we were put on to a Dakota which landed in Rangoon for refuelling and where we passed the night. The next morning very early we again boarded the Dakota bound for the airstrip at Naarn. The Japanese Air Force, which had once dominated the skies, seemed now to have been completely eliminated. I was dozing comfortably when, after a couple of hours, the co-pilot woke me and said, "Perhaps you could help us to find the strip. We only have a rough idea of where it might be. Would you come forward please?" I did as he said and was dismayed to see range after range of hills covered with jungle stretching into the distance. A lot of help I was going to be as the pilot's assistant! Looking round rather hopelessly, I suddenly saw, on the far horizon, the characteristic shape of the table-topped mountain where I had dreamed of situating a golf course! Full now of confidence I directed the pilot to the mountain and shortly afterwards we began our descent to Naarn.

David Smiley was waiting at the airstrip and while a good deal of useful material was being off loaded from the plane he told me how the briefcase had exploded. His arm had been unbandaged the night before we arrived by a Thai Air Force medical officer, who had removed some forty maggots from it. I exclaimed in horror at this episode, but the MO expressed his satisfaction that the maggots had eaten all the dead and putrefying flesh. The wound, he said, was now clean and would heal quickly! David returned in the Dakota to India where he stayed three weeks with the Viceroy to whom, I think, he was related. He then was dropped or landed in his original area of Thailand.

My first task was to contact the American officer. He was Major Alex Griswold to whom I had been given a "secret" introduction by a friend at Force 136 HQ. Why "secret" one may well ask. It was a very depressing fact that whereas in the European theatre of war the British and US clandestine services could hardly have co-operated more closely, in South-East Asia Command quite the opposite was the case. At the HQs of Force 136 and the corresponding American organization OSS (Office of Strategic Services) an apparent total distrust prevailed, at least officially. I went over to visit Alex at the airfield where he had made his headquarters.

It was not long before we were having a good laugh at our respective superiors (an exception must be made for Lt. Col. Poynton who was always supportive of our efforts). Alex told me that when leaving for Thailand he was briefed as to my presence and told that I was a particularly dangerous person! I was amazed to see Alex had brought a typewriter with him. "I'm only a desktop soldier," he explained. "I can't get on without my typewriter." He had also brought an NCO with him who seemed to have no prejudice against the Brits.

While I was away in Calcutta the Thai Air Force had built me a house at Khonsan. Entirely constructed of bamboo, it rested on stilts in the Thai style and was marvellously cool and airy and also free of some of the animals which tend to walk about at night in that part of the world. The Air Force always had a plane (one of the veteran biplanes of course) standing by to enable me to go to Naarn, or anywhere else for that matter.

It was now necessary to do some serious planning: the Japanese were in the process of being defeated in

Burma. In the face of the Allied domination of the air, they were unable to bring up supplies for their frontline troops. At the same time 14th Army was increasing its power. There had been times when it was struggling to prevent the Japanese from invading India. Kohima had marked the turning point and now it was the Imperial Army which was in retreat. The infamous Thailand–Burma railway, on which prisoners by the thousand had died through starvation or ill treatment, was now only marginally in operation or had been totally interrupted by Allied air strikes. It seemed only a question of time, probably quite a short time, before the Japanese would have to abandon Burma altogether. It seemed most unlikely that they would be able to create a front in Thailand. Evacuation by sea would surely prove impossible with the Allies in command of the air (the reverse of the situation, in fact, which culminated in the fall of Singapore). In all probability, so it seemed to Chew and me, with Alex concurring, the Japanese would be obliged to retreat through Thailand into Laos and Vietnam (then known as Indo-China) where at least the Mekong might provide a considerable obstacle to the advancing Allies.

We felt that we must take advantage of the fact that the whole area of north-east Thailand was free of the Japanese and that the Thais, presumably with a secret all clear from the Government in Bangkok were more than willing to help Force 136 and OSS. We were already being helped by the regional authorities and the Air Force. We did not as yet know how the Thai army might be disposed to act.

There were quite a few airstrips in the area, although some of them might be out of action at the height of the rainy season. There was also a substantial number of parachute dropping grounds where, apart from Phu Wiang, weapons could be landed without alerting too many neighbouring villages.

On careful consideration, the most likely line of retreat for the Japanese Army across Thailand appeared to be Kanchanaburi, west of Bangkok, Korat (Nakhon Ratchasima) and then towards Rolet or Yasothon, aiming to cross the Mekong at Savannakhet or Khemmarat. Cambodia would be another possibility, but that way would seem to lead the Japanese too far south.

We determined to aim at building up as large and well armed a force as possible in the area north-east of Khonkaen. Such a force should be able to pass through the hilly country between Khonkaen and Chaiyaphum and, dividing into small groups, sabotage and ambush the Japanese lines of communication. Then they would retreat into the hills and jungle. It was a sound principle that guerrilla bands should never confront enemy troops in face-to-face battle.

It was now a question of the RAF or USAF dropping or landing the greatest possible amount of weapons and explosives and of us distributing them and teaching the locals how to use them. About the middle of June we were lucky to obtain the expertise of Major Chris Blathwayte. Chris had already been in the Army (I forget his regiment but know that he wore black crowns on his shoulders — much superior to white crowns he gave me to understand!). He had then become a Jed and saw fierce fighting with the *maquisards* in Brittany. Afterwards he had volunteered for the Far East and we had travelled out to India on the *Otranto* where I had got to know him. Full of enthusiasm, he was just the man to operate our training programme. Very quickly he was installed at Phu Wiang and supplied with a drop of arms and explosives for use in demonstrations and for practice in ambush and sabotage operations.

Before long Chris had created a real school of guerrilla warfare. The community leaders (Nai Amphur) were given regular SOE-Jed training and then returned to their villages to organize and equip small groups ready for action.

One day I went with a guide across the wooded hills surrounding Phu Wiang. It was a surprisingly long and rough journey by a stony footpath through the jungle. I was pleased to see that Chris was well installed and his students seemed to be assimilating his teachings enthusiastically!

In addition to all the help which the Air Force gave us we benefited greatly from the co-operation of the provincial authorities, at Khonkaen where our special point of contact was the head of the Education Department and at Loei where our particular friend was the Chief of Police.

By about the first week of July '45 the development of our area was proceeding apace; we seemed to be operating under apparently peacetime conditions. Aeroplanes came and went, crossing the Burma front lines with absolute impunity. Brigadier Jacques, who had been hidden away by the Thai Government in the heart of Bangkok for months on end had, with the greatest secrecy, been smuggled out of Thailand to report on the general situation to Allied HQ in Calcutta. He returned via one of our airfields. An extremely affable and able man, he must have been well over six feet tall and also very thin. It was easy to see why the Thais had kept him under wraps. He and a senior Thai official stopped over at Khonsan before they proceeded by Thai Air Force plane to Bangkok.

Suddenly this tranquil situation was interrupted by an urgent message from Khonkaen: a group of Japanese officers was inspecting the area. They would land at Khonsan on the following day to meet the Thai Air Force officers there. Things certainly moved quickly after that. All the huts, including the one in which I was living, were emptied of everything which might show any connection with the Allies — radio sets, weapons, clothes, cigarettes. Also Chew, Noon and myself were despatched to some huts quite a distance from the airstrip. When the Japanese arrived all was clear. Presumably they were suitably entertained by the Thais and departed apparently satisfied that all was well. Why they had come we never knew, just a routine visit perhaps, or had something made them suspicious? One thing was sure — if they had known what was going on the Imperial Army still had the strength to make life very difficult for our embryo guerrilla forces.

Shortly afterwards I went to Korat (Nakhon Ratchasima). The purpose of my visit was to sound out the General in command of the Thai Army in the area of north-east Thailand. We knew from our friends in the Air Force that the Army was likely to be friendly to the Allies, but we had no idea what forces they might have or how they might be prepared to use them in support of our plan of campaign.

Taking off from Khonsan we flew over the area from which we envisaged our guerrillas attacking the Japanese on their retreat towards Indo-China. There were plenty of wooded hills and jungle into which small groups of men could stage an ambush and simply disappear.

The Thai officers received us in the friendliest way. The commanding General was just so nice one could have hugged him! He said that the Thai Army based on Korat would help us in any way they could. I asked how many men it consisted of. The General replied that he had approximately 7000 men under his command! This was an army. I had reckoned that the guerrillas of the north-east would only consist of a few hundred men operating in small groups. What to do with the 7000? Moreover, they were in the wrong place. Korat itself would lie right in the path of the Japanese Army coming in the direction of Bangkok and making for the crossings of the Mekong at Savannakhet, Khemmarat or Ubon/Pakse. Even if the Thais did nothing Korat would be a dangerous place to be. I wondered whether we could take some men from the army and incorporate them into the guerrilla units we were forming in the area centred on Khonsan. We would have to look at the situation when I returned there. In the meantime I thanked the General for his offer and said that I would come back with a plan of action in a week or two.

During the two or three days that I was in Korat the Thai police brought three Frenchmen to the Army HQ. They were parachutists who had been on their way to organize or reinforce the French Vietnamese resistance to the Japanese somewhere in what had been French Indo-China. Something had gone wrong with the plane which had been carrying them and they had been obliged to jump as quickly as possible, regardless of where they might land. As it happened, they had landed in Thailand not far from the border with Cambodia (also pre-war under French rule). They had been arrested by the Thai police who had taken them to Korat. They were now handed over to me. They were rather surprised to find that a shaving brush, which I lent them to shave their rather copious beards, had been bought in Le Mans the year before! We eventually got them back to Naarn and put them on one of the RAF Dakotas which were now landing there almost as a matter of routine.

We returned to Khonsan by the same aerial route as we had come. As I was looking over the side of the plane at the terrain of jungle below the slipstream of the plane suddenly tore off one of my shoulder badges. From then on I was able to sport only one crown. Well, one would just have to do!

The build-up was continuing. Chris Blathwayte's school at Phu Wiang seemed to be going strong. Then, sadly, we had our first casualty. The Nai Ampur (District Officer) of one of our districts had been to

Chris's school and was instructing some of the men in the village of which he was in charge in the use of grenades. The grenade which he was using was the standard British army type in which a lever was used to hold a spring. When thrown the lever came off, the spring would activate the striker which would cause the grenade to explode after five seconds, spraying fragments of iron over a wide area. It was known that occasionally, only very occasionally, the grenade would not go off, in which case the instructor would leave it for five minutes then place next to it a charge with a one minute fuse attached, take cover and let the charge explode the grenade. The Nai Ampur was apparently carrying out these instructions when the grenade suddenly exploded, killing him instantly.

During this time I kept in regular touch with Alex Griswold, who, independently of Force 136, but strategically co-ordinating his activities with ours, was continuing to receive weapons and explosives. Chew and I continued to live at the Thai Air Force HQ and Noon had his radio set nearby, with which he was in day-to-day communication with Calcutta.

Living was remarkably pleasant in spite of the heat. In the first days after my second incursion into Thailand I had acquired an extremely unpleasant heat rash. I had the idea of sunbathing (now frowned upon by the medical profession). Within days the rash had totally disappeared and was replaced by a fine shade of brown.

All of us British and Americans in our short time in Thailand had developed a considerable admiration for the Thai people. As they had never been subject to a colonial power, they did not have the same ambivalence towards Europeans and Americans which so often characterized the other peoples of Southern Asia. They hated the Japanese who had occupied their country and certainly welcomed us in our role as co-ordinators of resistance and suppliers of weapons, which would help them get rid of their enemy. The Thais had also a marvellous charm, all the more striking in that all our friends and colleagues were exclusively male. None of us British or Americans had ever seen a Thai woman. A woman in the Thai language is a "poo ying". Probably Alex's NCO expressed something on behalf of all of us Anglo-Saxons when he remarked, somewhat plaintively, "I wanna see a poo ying"!

By the end of July the development of our guerrilla army area between Khonkaen and Loei seemed to be proceeding according to plan. When I took off from Khonsan in my biplane for a routine visit to Loei I felt quite pleased with what we had achieved.

CHAPTER TWELVE

After the Japanese Surrender

It must have been about 5 August that a large drop of arms was scheduled to take place on a savannah some 10 kms north of Khonsan. It was to be a big drop — four planeloads Calcutta informed us. We sent a radio message confirming that we would be awaiting the planes at the dropping ground — named "Kanaka". Shortly afterwards we received a message from HQ Calcutta worded approximately as follows: "Your 5/8 received in clear repeat in clear. Regret must cancel drop to Kanaka. Please report any Japanese planes which might be over site at day and time of planned drop." To say we were dumfounded would be an understatement. It was evident that in some lapse of mind our hitherto totally reliable radio operator Noon had simply omitted to code the message. We apologized profusely for his mistake and asked Calcutta for their forgiveness. We also informed them that the Japanese had not been seen anywhere near "Kanaka" either in the air or on the ground. HQ replied generously forgiving us and Noon for the non-coded message and strangely adding "Hope Atom bomb will have blasted Japanese memories". We were certainly puzzled at this curious sentence but found no solution as to what it might mean. That evening, listening to the BBC news, we soon realized that a devastating blow had been struck against the Japanese heartland.

During the next days the military situation appeared unchanged. It still seemed probable that the Japanese Army would have to retreat from Burma via Thailand. Then came the news of the second atom bomb upon Nagasaki. Soon after we heard the incredible announcement that Japan had totally capitulated.

I have to confess to extraordinarily mixed feelings at this moment of Allied triumph. On the one hand there was an inescapable element of disappointment. All we had planned, all the weapons and explosives that had been landed or dropped by parachute, all the men who had been recruited from the local population and trained to be a fighting force, all the devoted cooperation of the Thai Air force and the civil authorities, all seemed to be for nothing. On the other hand if we had attacked the Japanese army in retreat across Thailand there would surely have been many casualties. Even if the guerrilla bands had been able to make good their escape into the hills and jungles, the civilian population would have suffered the vengeful reprisals of the Imperial Army.

It was afterwards discovered that orders had been issued to the commanders of the Japanese forces in Thailand that in the eventuality of an Allied attack all prisoners of war and their Korean guards were to be exterminated immediately, without exception. It is unlikely that the fate of the Thai population of the towns and villages along the line of the Japanese retreat, whence our guerrilla bands were to be drawn, would have been any different. Terrible decisions would have had to be taken. Anyway, it was all over now.

After a day or two a Dakota brought us friends and all the news. Alex Griswold, Chew and I were instructed to proceed to Korat. There we were to meet a group of Japanese officers who, under Allied direction, would accompany us by train to Ubon Ratchathani. Not far from the town there was known to be a large prisoner-of-war camp. The prisoners were the survivors of the men who had worked on the Thailand to Burma railway.

It was in the evening on the station platform at Korat that we met the Japanese. Although they had been prepared for the encounter, they were apparently surprised by the presence of armed men in Allied uniforms at such a distance behind their front lines. The meeting was stiff, to say the least, Alex ever polite, murmured something like, "Pleased to meet you"! I looked at them with as much hostility as I could muster and said nothing.

We then embarked on the night train for Ubon, a distance of about 220 kms. The train was rather slow and stopped at several stations but it was remarkable that it was running at all. The railway authority had provided for the comfort of its distinguished passengers by giving them each one side of a compartment so that they were able to stretch out. However, they had not thought to segregate Allied and Japanese officers. So it was that my travelling companion was a Japanese Captain or Major. It was difficult to put up the barrier of dignified hauteur which I had felt appropriate for the meeting on the platform in the enforced intimacy of a whole night in a railway compartment. However, the fact that neither of us was able to speak a word of the other's language made for our maintaining a certain distance.

On our arrival in a somewhat unshaven and dishevelled state at Ubon station, we were joined by David Smiley and proceeded in two trucks provided by the provincial Governor to the POW camp. We had seen photographs of prisoners freed from the German concentration camps and knew something of the terrible conditions to which the POWs had been subject in Japanese camps, and particularly what they had had to endure on the Thailand-Burma railway. Approaching the Ubon camp we braced ourselves for the anticipated shock of finding men at the limits of survival.

We drove up to the entrance to the camp. The Japanese guards were nowhere to be seen. At the gate stood two sentries in immaculate British tropical uniforms. They saluted us smartly and to our astonished enquiry as to who might be in charge one of them replied, "The Colonel asked me to take you to the orderly room, sir." Sure enough we accompanied the soldier to the orderly room where, surrounded by his staff, Lt. Col Philip Toosey stood ready to receive us.

It was a show-off of course, but what a show-off! Toosey, as I recall, offered us a cup of tea and then told us how it had happened. The railway had indeed been a nightmare. It was reckoned that some two-thirds of the Allied POWs (nearly all British and Australian) captured at the fall of Singapore had died of privations and disease. Toosey had been responsible for some alleviation in the régime of near starvation and beatings at the slightest provocation, real or imagined, by the guards. He had pointed out to the Japanese commandant that the prisoners would work better if they were allowed to organize their work themselves without being subject to continual interference.

When the railway had been completed in 1943 the POWs had been dispersed. The Ubon camp held about 3000 of them, mainly officers. Conditions were certainly better than on the railway although hunger was an ever-present condition of life. The men told us that the Japanese guards in an effort to keep down the swarms of flies offered a tin of rice as a reward to the prisoners who would collect a jar of the creatures. This worked so well that a few POWs who had some contact with the local Thai population actually managed to get them to supply quantities of flies. Flies = rice was the equation which, on occasion, helped the POWs to eke out their ration to the mystification of the Thais.

Toosey told us that once the Japanese had heard of the surrender they had immediately released all the Red Cross parcels which had been destined for the POWs and which the guards had been storing for months. Some of these had contained uniforms. Hence the impressive appearance of the sentries and the members of the orderly room.

The Colonel then ordered all the men out on parade, introduced us and then just let us mingle with the crowd. It was an emotional moment for us all.

The next few days were spent in helping to get matters organized for the ex-POWs before they could be evacuated. We received by air an army doctor, a radio operator, a sergeant and a corporal, all members of the Parachute Regiment. Rice we were able to provide locally, bully beef and suchlike eatables were carried by the planes which gradually began to evacuate the POWs, British, Australian and Dutch. They were all thin but in surprisingly good condition. Apparently only the toughest had survived the hardships of the railway and these had taken on a new lease of life in the relatively improved conditions of the Ubon camp. There were many accounts of the brutalities inflicted by the Japanese and the Korean conscripts in the Imperial Army on the POWs. There was one particular tale, however, which shed a curious light on the Japanese attitude to life. A number of Japanese casualties had been evacuated from Burma to Thailand and were lying in a piteous condition, moaning for water. One or two of the POWs were so moved by this situation that they attempted to bring the wounded men a tin or two of water. Their guards restrained them. The POWs, I suppose through an interpreter, pointed out that the men were their own soldiers. "Leave them alone," came the reply, "They have broken their oath to the Emperor to die in battle rather than leave the front."

While we were in Ubon we received a message telling us that David and I were promoted to Lt. Col. Shortly afterwards a friend brought the appropriate shoulder badges. I no longer had to wear my single crown. Chew became a Major at the same time. When it was clear that there was nothing further that we could usefully do in Ubon to help to provide for the ex POWs now in rapid process of evacuation, Chew and I decided to return to north-east Thailand to thank all those who had been so helpful to our mission in the preceding months. This turned out to be one of the most exhausting episodes I have ever experienced. The Thais (male and female this time!) involved us in a programme of visits and more especially banquets which must have lasted for about ten days. They could not have been more friendly, apparently appreciative of what we had done and displaying the most touching hospitality.

After a very pleasant reception and an overnight stay in Khonkaen we set off for Phu Wiang, the location of our training school. After about 40 kms of road travel, in the usual trucks, on the way to Khonsan and Loei, we came to the track leading to Phu Wiang. It was too rough for any vehicle and our hosts had kindly provided horses. My last attempt at riding had been at the age of five. Even then I realized that this form of locomotion was not for me. Well, I just had to face it — 30 kms by Thai horse to Phu Wiang! When we eventually reached the village I was absolutely done in; so was the horse, and we parted without regret! Then, a quick wash and brush up and on to the next banquet.

We left Phu Wiang, a true Shangri La it seemed, by a footpath through the hills. We were picked up by truck and taken to Khonsan for more celebrations. Our final stopover was Loei. I particularly remember the banquet there. It started with a suckling pig, barbecued over a fire. The crackling was absolutely delicious. As I was savouring some of it the Nai Ampur came up to me with a pleasant looking young woman and startled me by saying in English, "Your wife"! What should I do in these circumstances I wondered. The young woman duly took the place next to mine at the succeeding banquet. I should explain that I had by now acquired quite a vocabulary of Thai words and was even able to maintain a sort of conversation. I also found that it was unnecessary to make jokes as my pronunciation of the right word to convey my meaning but on the wrong tone was, at times, so funny as to stretch even Thai politeness to its limit! At any rate I was able to use all my vocabulary in friendly conversation with "my wife". She did not seem to expect any further attention and we parted very amiably. However, the following evening was another banquet and there she was, sitting next to me again — with all my vocabulary exhausted the previous evening.

We returned to Khonkhaen and stayed three days, visiting and sightseeing. One of our companions was a young Thai woman (another!). I spent one day talking my kind of Thai to her. The following day I discovered that she was a teacher of English! Our farewells to the area completed, the Thai Air Force took us to Korat. Thence a RAF plane flew us to Bangkok.

The city was in a state of celebration at the defeat of the hated Japanese. It was not only the quasi-occupation of their country for which the Thais disliked the Japanese, but their arrogance. The soldiers of the Imperial Army appeared to have carried the concept of *Herrenvolk* to an extreme at least equal to that of the Nazis. No wonder that in "the land of the free" they were not popular!

In Bangkok I joined a number of friends from Force 136, some from the Calcutta office, some who had been behind the lines in Burma. It was soon after my arrival that I was delegated as a guest of honour to watch the celebratory parade of the Thai armed forces. They certainly put on quite a show. I was glad to see Major Chew and Captain Noon, among other old friends, proudly marching past.

The following two or three weeks was spent mainly in partying. The Thais were more than generous in their hospitality towards the Allied officers, of which there were now quite a few in Bangkok. The city had become the Allied HQ in the complicated tasks of getting the ex-POWs home and repatriating the Japanese army, with the exception of those who could be regarded as war criminals or guilty of crimes against humanity and, finally, transporting the soldiers of the 14th Army and their Allies back to their respective homelands. Two incidents stand out in my memory from this period.

Some Thai friends took me to see an exhibition of Thai boxing. Strong and very supple young men performed extraordinary feats of kicking each other in different parts of their anatomies. Then a grey-haired mature-looking gentleman came on the scene. I thought the young men would make short work of him. As it was he made short work of them, kicking them all over the place. I would have seen more of the show, but as I was watching I suddenly began to feel queasy and then rapidly queasier and queasier! I asked one of my friends to get me back to my hotel, feeling worse and worse, just made it to my room and was sick as a dog! Talking of dogs, but not sick ones, I noticed when looking out of my hotel room in the early morning that what I can only describe as a dogs' general meeting took place every day. I counted eighteen of them at one such session. Unlike the dogs in India which are mostly in an absolutely pathetic condition, these dogs looked perfectly healthy. I commented on this to Chew with whom I continued to be in touch. "All quite normal," he assured me. "There is always plenty to eat in Thailand."

It dawned on me that this was perhaps the key to the Thai attitude to life. The charm which had so impressed all of us who had lived even a short time in Thailand was perhaps due to the absence of social pressure or stress (so much blamed for the ills of Western society). In this Southern Buddhist culture, there lay an element of insouciance, culminating in the philosophy of detachment from the chains of life.

It was at this time that I was invited to a small dinner party given by my old friend Chin and the then Mayor of Bangkok. I found myself sitting next to an extremely pretty Thai girl whom I was able to regale with the increasing number of Thai phrases which I had learnt.

The food was superb and absolutely Chinese. (All the best restaurants in Bangkok in those days were Chinese.) When we had finished the innumerable courses, amidst the general jollity, it was explained to me that the young lady whom I had been sitting next to, would be happy to invite me to her house for the night. Indeed I would be welcome to stay there for the rest of the time I might be in Bangkok. Khun X was in fact a courtesan — her looks and grace were certainly outstanding. Chin and the Mayor had obviously been at pains to select this delightful creature for me as a token of appreciation for my work in Thailand.

I will admit to a considerable degree of inner conflict over what I was to do next. However, in the end, and to the amazement of my friends, including Khun X, I said I must decline their very kind offer. "Courtesans," I said, "were the exploitation of woman by man with which my principles just wouldn't agree!" In the end they drove off leaving me rather sadly at the door of my hotel.

I think they all respected me more than if I had accepted Khun X's invitation. Not because of any moral scruple but because I had shown an insouciance to physical pleasure. Chin and the Mayor certainly bore me no ill will and I often shared a joke with Khun X whom I saw afterwards on several occasions and who had been allocated to another Allied officer.

While I was in Bangkok Chris Blathwayte had been posted to the town of Pakse in Laos. His mission, rather vaguely defined, was to liaise with the French who had been dropped in the area some time prior to Armistice and were now in nominal control. There was also a detachment of one hundred and fifty Japanese awaiting repatriation. With Chris was a radio operator. It must have been around the middle of September '45 that some messages from Chris became somewhat garbled and the advanced HQ of Force 136, now in Bangkok, felt that all was not well. In fact Chris had caught one of the local bugs and was running a temperature nearing 40 degrees C at the time! As I had time on my hands after the various proceedings in north-east Thailand and, one might say, had a general interest in France, I volunteered to go to Pakse and see what was going on there. The RAF kindly flew me to Ubon — the POWs had effectively been evacuated by this time — and on to Pakse.

I found that Chris had more or less recovered from his fever and was now locked in disagreement with the French officers, the leaders of whom were Commandant Legrand and Captain J.M. de Gannay, also old friends from Force 136. The problem, trivial on the face of it, was that one of the local community leaders, a vet by profession, said that he had been bitten by a rabid dog. As the only available vaccine was in Saigon, he requested that he might travel there as soon as possible. Chris felt that he should go, but the French thought that the only object of his journey was to inform the dissident Vietnamese regarding the situation in the Bas Laos, as the region around Pakse was then known. It should be explained that the French were at that time by no means in control of Saigon and what would later become the Vietnamese resistance to the French was already beginning to be active. I found that, curiously, my French friends and colleagues seemed to have a remarkable respect for rank. As I was the only Lieut. Colonel around it followed that everybody would do what I told them. This included the French, the Laotians, and of course, the Japanese. What a situation! Needless to say that, with the most altruistic of intentions, I decided to take full advantage of it!

I at once had a talk with the vet. It seemed probable that the French were right and that his object in going to Saigon was to report on the situation in Pakse. So what? I decided to back Chris' opinion. The French thought we were wrong but insisted in deferring to my judgement. The vet stayed for two or three days to see what we were doing and then left, I thought rather reluctantly, but he had tied himself in with his account of the rabid dog bite.

Pakse seemed to have no central authority at all. What to do? I have mentioned that I had an aunt who was Mayor of Eastbourne. Staying with her, she often told me about the proceedings of the Town Council of which she was an Alderman. Obviously what Pakse needed was a Town Council! There were several communities in the area: Laotian, Vietnamese, Chinese were the main groups. With a little local advice and putting out some feelers, I invited two or three members of each community to come to a meeting. We appointed an elderly and apparently much respected Lao gentleman as the Chairman and there was the

Town Council of Pakse! I appointed myself Adviser to the Chairman!

Most of the doings of the Council (and its Adviser) are lost in the mists of time. However, a few incidents stand out in my memory. The first problem was to obtain something to eat for the population. Due to the war and the fact that the rice harvest was not yet in, food was very scarce. The Japanese seemed to have plenty so I requisitioned 300 tonnes of rice from their stores. The Council distributed it, so all at once it became very popular!

The next problem was not one for the Council. Chris and I had been joined by another SOE agent, Harry Despaigne, and the Sergeant and the Corporal who had been involved in evacuating the POW camp in Ubon. We now heard by a radio message from Bangkok that the Allies had agreed with the Chinese that the latter's zone of occupation was to be north of the 16th parallel, about 100 kms north of Pakse. It was thought to be a good idea to establish some kind of presence at the parallel before the Chinese could cross it. We had already heard that the Chinese Army had entered Laos and the Chinese community in Pakse were getting ready to welcome it. Certainly once the Chinese had crossed the officially agreed line there would be little to stop them anywhere in Indo-China. We must do something to mark the limit to their zone of occupation.

We immediately and unofficially promoted our Sergeant to Captain, the Corporal to Lieutenant and then dressed about fifteen Laotian soldiers in British uniforms. These had been landed by the RAF together with a jeep and other useful material. We then commandeered a motor-ship in the Pakse "harbour", put our "troops" on it, added one or two interpreters and ordered them all to travel to the 16th parallel and disembark there. The "troops" would then set up a kind of frontier post with various Allied flags and object as strongly as possible if the Chinese army should go past it. As it happened, the Chinese did not attempt to cross the 16th parallel. Did they perhaps know that the Allies had so clearly marked the frontier of their zone of occupation?

Not long after we had established the frontier post a curious incident took place. A French woman and her son, aged about twelve, who had been living in Pakse as refugees were to be repatriated. At that time we only had available a Thai Air Force plane. The pilot said that he would take the two to Korat where they could surely find transport to Bangkok. They set off one afternoon but, as we heard by radio, never arrived. It was a matter of considerable anxiety, wondering what could have happened to them. Then the Frontier post at the 16th parallel came through on the radio. No need to worry. The pilot had lost his way completely; it was getting dark and he was running out of fuel. He decided to ditch in the Mekong River. The pilot, the woman and the boy had swum ashore and were being looked after at the post. The plane had disappeared into the Mekong!

Chris and I and a few friends decided to take the little ship which was lying in the harbour at Pakse and go up river to the 16th parallel. We would take some supplies for the "troops", see generally what was going on and then return to Pakse. I was astonished and impressed by the Mekong. The river is about 2 kms wide at Pakse and apparently is the same width at Vientiane on the northern Thailand-Laos border. In the valley south of Khemmarat the hills on each side narrow the Mekong to maybe 200 metres and the flow of the swirling current was correspondingly increased. Our ship could hardly make headway against it. The post had been made quite effective looking. Anybody could see that south of this point the Allies were in command! In fact, it seemed that the Chinese Army had halted its southward march around Savannakhet. Perhaps they had heard about our post. The Chinese community in Pakse were disappointed, but everyone else was much relieved. We took the three who had swum ashore in the Mekong back with us. They were all rather quiet!

The repatriation of the Japanese was the next problem which had to be dealt with. We understood that some of the remnants of the Imperial Army were being concentrated at Phnom Penh. Once more we requisitioned a ship and the Japanese soldiers in Pakse were ordered to prepare to board it. On the eve of their departure our Dutch-, English- and Japanese-speaking interpreter told us that the men, though otherwise pleased enough to go, were much distressed at their Captain ordering them to leave their pet peacock behind. He added that the Captain, Hashimoto by name, was proposing to commit suicide (hara-kiri) on his return to Japan, thus atoning for the shame of defeat. Chris and I resolved to visit Captain Hashimoto. The interpreter made a date and we set off in our Jeep (the RAF had kindly landed one of these marvellous vehicles for us a couple of weeks before). We had removed our shoulder badges to show that this was not an official call and were duly shown into the Captain's room by an orderly. He politely asked us if we would care for a cup of chocolate. We said yes and a curious ceremony then ensued. The orderly with the chocolate stood at the door of the room wearing a face mask and, according to the interpreter, said loudly, "I am outside the door". He then came in and said, "I am inside the door." He kept on his mask while pouring the chocolate. After a few politenesses, I made a kind of speech, pausing at intervals for the interpreter to translate. As I recall it, what I said was more or less as follows:

> The war was over now and I had heard that some of the Japanese officers were thinking of committing suicide when they had supervised the transport of their men back to Japan. Now I wished to say this: — there were no braver soldiers that the Japanese. We had courageous soldiers too and (bringing in Chris) we also knew that the Germans were fine fighters but the Japanese were the equal of them all. They had lost the war because of the overpowering forces set against them. And then the atom bomb . . . The stain on their reputation was of course their treatment of

the prisoners of war. Now we had, all of us, to deal with rebuilding the world. We must look to the future — not any more to the past.

Captain Hashimoto listened in silence until the interpreter had finished translating. Then he said that he could never have imagined that he would hear anything like the ideas I had expressed coming from an Allied officer. He was certainly impressed. He also accepted that those who had ill-treated POWs should be punished. Chris and I continued the conversation for a short while. Then, before taking our leave; I said that we had heard that his men were very devoted to a peacock which, on their departure from Pakse, they were being told to leave behind. I would ask him (I was careful not to say "order") to allow them to take the peacock on the ship. The Captain really managed a smile at this request and agreed that the peacock could accompany the soldiers! A day or two later the Japanese, and the peacock, departed by ship down the Mekong.

A new difficulty now arose which was certainly beyond the Town Council to solve. This involved salt. The diet of the inhabitants of Pakse and its neighbouring province consisted largely of fish of which there were apparently plenty to be obtained from the river. In order to preserve their catches, the fishermen normally proceeded to salt them. However, owing to the dislocation of the economy of Indo-China, it was now unobtainable.

The nearest possible source of supply was said to be at Ubon in Thailand. How to obtain it? About three weeks into my stay in Pakse I went to Bangkok to report to HQ on how matters were proceeding in Pakse and took the opportunity to call on a rather senior Thai Government official and explained the problem. He was sympathetic and said if the Ka-Luang (Governor) of Pakse would get in touch with the Ka-Luang of Ubon he should be able to release some salt. Proudly I said, "I am the Ka-Luang of Pakse." "In that case," he said with mild amusement, "Perhaps we can settle it together." In the end I bought 50 tonnes of salt to be sent by road and river from Ubon to Pakse. I forget the sum involved but I do remember the rumpus — there is no other word for it — which was caused by the piastre slipping in value relative to the baht between the time the salt was purchased and the time we came to pay for it. The exchange rate had been 1 to 1 and had now become 1.3 to 1. I felt that the difference should be made up by HM Government as a contribution to the peace of the area. It was eventually paid. Fifty years later my friend Harvey Bathurst of Force 136 told me he had not forgotten the trouble it gave him.

The Laotians are a remarkably gentle and polite people. It was disconcerting at first to find grown men with whom we had no contact giving one a formal bow. Perhaps it was the French who had taught them to show due respect to their undeserving white masters. I was anxious to show that, post-war, a more egalitarian attitude should prevail. Henceforth, whenever any one in the street bowed to me, I gave them a smart salute in the best style of the Royal Fusiliers. Their way of life and Buddhist philosophical outlook was even more marked than in neighbouring Thailand. It surely made them particularly vulnerable to exploitation by more aggressive people — European or Chinese. In fact the Chinese community invited Chris and me to a superb meal. Proudly they pointed to a fairly elderly but by no means ancient gentleman. He had, they said, been the first Chinese to install himself as a shopkeeper in Pakse. By 1945 they dominated all trade.

My de facto tenure of office as Governor of Pakse came to an end after about six weeks with the arrival of the official appointee of the French Government. This was of course what we had expected. I will admit, however, to a sense of disappointment in the man who, in effect, I was handing over to. A worthy fellow, he had spent the entire period of the war in Chandenagore, a town in India which was one of five *comptoirs* which were under French rule. He obviously was going by the principle that everything in Indo-China was to be restored exactly as it had been before the war. He seemed not to appreciate that the days of the white man as a god were over.

We were sad to leave Pakse. In a short time we had made many friends. At the last moment, one of them, a *père blanc* who had a parish in the country near Pakse, approached me and said his "*voisinage pullule de tigres*" and would we give him a gun. I left him an old British army rifle with which he was delighted and said, "*Tout le monde dit du bien de vous.*"

The little plane rose over the vastness of the Mekong. Maybe something good remained of our stay in Pakse.

I spent the next three months in Bangkok being invited to parties and seeing many places of interest. But it was the Thai people, the attitude to life and the Buddhist religion — philosophy, I feel really is a better word — which I found completely fascinating. That they were able to enjoy the normal pleasures of life whilst at the same time retaining a slight measure of detachment (I have called it "insouciance") made for a particularly attractive culture. It seemed true that this detachment contained a degree of fatalism which could at times be a hindrance to action. It was a question as to how the Thais would evolve in the post-war world. They had marvellously avoided colonization by the European powers and they had to some extent assimilated a large number of Chinese immigrants into the indigent population. Yet it was evident that post-war exposure to European and US influence was going to result in many changes in the Thai way of life and in much industrial development. I felt that I would like to be part of this process and that I might be able to contribute something to it.

The Head of the Government at the time — he had been Regent and later Prime Minister — was Luang Pradit (Pridi Panomyong). As a member of Force 136 and indeed a member of the Thai resistance which he had led, I had quite easy access to him. He was an extremely pleasant personality and had studied law in France and even practiced as a lawyer in Caen. He spoke French and English with great fluency. He appeared to have an idealistic view of the future of his country. I told him that I was fascinated by Thailand and that when I was demobilized I would like to come back to it and assist in its development. Chin, who was now living in Bangkok and who was in close touch with Pradit, strongly supported me in this project. Pradit was quite welcoming. He said that if I would get in touch with him when I had been demobilized he would certainly see what he could do.

Early in 1946 a tragic incident took place. The young King of Thailand was being educated with his brother in Switzerland. (It was said that he produced an outstanding essay on the Cantonal Constitution of the Confederation.) Not long after the end of the war and the final departure of the Japanese he returned to Thailand amidst general rejoicing. All appeared to be going well and it seemed probable that he would be a very popular constitutional monarch. His Swiss upbringing would have ensured a penchant for a modern way of life.

One morning a servant going into his room to wake him was shocked and amazed to find the young Kind dead. He had been shot through the head and a pistol lay beside him. How and for what reason it had happened was a mystery. There was no evidence to implicate anyone. Just playing with his pistol perhaps, or, an eventuality totally unacceptable to the Thais, had he perhaps committed suicide?

Although Pradit could not possibly have been to blame in the affair of the King's death, it was a fact that from that day onwards his influence began steadily to wane. It was a long time before I gave up all hope of some kind of career in Thailand. I still wonder occasionally what part I might have played in the many developments of that nation (not all of them perhaps desirable) since 1946.

Finally, in February 1946, the news came that I was to be repatriated and demobilized. I bade farewell to my many Thai friends, hoping to see them again before long and was flown by RAF transport to Calcutta. I spent two or three days there accommodated in a pleasant bungalow, waiting for the next move to Karachi.

I remember going on a short shopping expedition in one of the markets and returning with a small parcel. (I have no idea what was in it.) A young man accosted me and in passable English offered to carry the parcel — for an anna or two, of course. I firmly declined his *offer*. He insisted, saying that I was "rajah-men" and should not carry anything. To his considerable amusement I explained to him that all men were now equal and "rajah-men" didn't exist any more. In the end I got into a taxi (not a rickshaw, it was against my principles to be pulled by a human being) and returned to my bungalow.

Karachi was my next stop. This time the airport accommodation consisted of bunks one above the other and was known to its inhabitants as "Belsen". Fortunately we were soon on the next stage of our journey. There was a fuelling stop in Tripoli and then we headed for London. This was quite an experience.

We must have been flying at 15000 feet when the plane's heating failed completely. In February, coming from the tropics, it felt remarkably chilly. The breath froze on our coats and I thought one of my fellow-passengers was going to collapse. The pilot took pity on us (perhaps also on his crew!) and descended to 5000 feet which was a slight improvement. We ended up by being driven across London in an open truck to the Chelsea barracks late at night.

The following morning I was given my official demobilization papers and proceeded to Olympia where I was allowed to choose a shirt, a jacket and a pair of trousers. These were put into a cardboard box and with that and a kit-bag I walked out of Olympia — a civilian! In a state of mild euphoria I took the District line to Turnham Green and then by taxi to where my parents were living in a rented flat. It was less than six years since the day I had reported to the barracks of the Royal Fusiliers in Hounslow. A lot had happened in between!

CHAPTER THIRTEEN

In Germany

In May 1946 my family and I travelled from Britain to Switzerland. For us all there was a fine sense of exhilaration in the journey. First the unobstructed journey across France, a night in the train and then the entry into Switzerland in the early morning, the train swinging down the long curves to Lausanne, in the background the mountains of Savoy and the Dents du Midi high above the blue of Lake Leman. Everything unchanged through all the years of war, suffering and death. Then there was our office in Lutry, just outside Lausanne, the people who had worked with us, our other friends and acquaintances, again all apparently unchanged. How glad they were that the Allies had won the war. (We discovered later that, though their pleasure at the defeat of the Axis was undoubtedly real, the sympathies of the Swiss had not prevented them from putting their industry, even to the smallest workshops, at the service of Hitler's war-machine.) Then they told us how much they had suffered — "The rationing and the air-raids, Monsieur". "But I thought you had never experienced any air-raids?" I enquired. "No, but the alarms . . ." Then there was one man, of the greatest respectability, who complained of the lack of golf balls, and, can you imagine it, they had to go to the golf club on bicycles. On a personal note, I may add, that chocolate rationing had just been abolished as we arrived in Switzerland. I limited myself to a *plaque* of 250 grammes per day!

We went up to our chalet at a place called Villars-sur-Ollon; there was the most marvellous view of the Alps. How unchanged it seemed since that day in 1939 when I had returned with the prize I had won at the Swiss Open. In our office in Lutry I began to help my father in picking up the pieces of the family business. Part of this consisted of acting as agents for ICI in the wholesale of industrial chemicals. The other part was composed of water-softening plant, de-scaling boilers and specialized chemicals for water treatment.

It was not long before I came face to face with the fact that this way of life, one with which I had been quite satisfied before September 1939, was now simply no longer tolerable. I think there are several reasons for this rather sad state of mind which impelled me to leave my family and our business just as my father was endeavouring to reconstitute it. I stayed in Switzerland for a year, during which time I became increasingly dissatisfied and depressed, and then handed my job over to my brother-in-law (also a former member of SOE Italian Section) who seemed quite pleased to take it. I left Switzerland in May 1947.

I returned to the UK, in a way depressed at all that I was leaving behind, and yet I could not rid myself of a sense of elation at somehow embarking on a new and, as I hoped, more idealistic way of life. Perhaps I thought of it as idealistic or was it simply that living in Switzerland was now too dull for me? I had also acquired a somewhat absurd measure of self-confidence. What was I doing selling chemicals on behalf of ICI when I might be influencing the Germans towards their own improvement? What was not obvious to me, but probably was to everybody else, was that my various experiences had made me more than a trifle off-balance! Probably most men and women had had their personalities changed over the war years and the operational members of SOE more than most.

I was fortunate in having a friend who was the Religious Affairs Adviser to the Control Commission for Germany. He gave me a recommendation to the recruitment section. I was duly interviewed and shortly afterwards found myself on a five-day briefing course. Curiously enough this took place at Bletchley which had been the headquarters of SOE's secret coding and decoding organization in earlier years. Due to my pre-war business background, I found myself posted to the Commerce Division in the Berlin offices of the Control Commission.

I travelled out to Germany in the Control Commission special train via the Hook of Holland. Soon after crossing the Dutch–German frontier we got a sight of the German towns and cities. The train went through Dusseldorf, Essen and the Ruhr. The scenes of devastation were unbelievable. What had once been factories — many of them turning out armaments — were now shattered ruins with only some of the walls still standing. In the residential areas of the city-centres people were living in the cellars underneath the ruins of their homes. Churchill had talked of "retribution". From the windows of the train I could see how this retribution had been executed. The train stopped at Essen, Bochum, Dortmund; on the platforms were Germans, seedy, hungry-looking and shabby. How different from the officers of the *Kommandantur* who had ruled Le Mans in the days of the Occupation.

The CCG train stopped for a time outside Hamm station. It was not long before it was besieged by children begging. Some of them, I noticed, were trying to sell Iron Crosses. These would have been earned in battle by the soldiers of the Third Reich. I could not help wondering, if Hitler had succeeded in his planned invasion of Britain, would British children have lined the railtracks at Clapham Junction selling MCs and DFCs for Reichmarks to buy bread on the black market. How the Germans must surely hate us as we would have hated them.

We stopped for the night in Herford. It was a small place apparently well known for making furniture and had been spared the Allied destruction of the industrial towns. Now it had become the headquarters of some units of the Control Commission. The next day we travelled to Berlin, crossing the border into the Russian zone of occupation and finally reaching the British sector of the city.

Berlin was an extraordinary sight. Standing in the centre was the Tiergarten which we had often seen on cinema newsreels with Hitler reviewing his troops, one could almost believe that the buildings one was seeing were standing intact. Moving a little closer, it was a shock to see that every single one of them was a burnt-out shell with only the walls still standing. The destruction of Berlin had been carried out with incendiary bombs. There seemed to be no effort at reconstruction. This was August 1947 and only a few gangs of people, mainly women, were clearing rubble by hand and shovel.

I was allocated quite a pleasant room in a requisitioned building in a suburb of Berlin. Meals were in a CCG Mess. The next day I reported to HQ Commerce Division where I was immediately in for a rather unpleasant surprise. I had my first interview with the Deputy Head of the Division, a pleasant enough man who had formerly been a senior RAF officer. After a few minutes he said, "I hope you're not an idealist." I forbore replying that I hoped that this was just what I was. My enthusiasm somewhat cooled by this incident, I began to meet some of my fellow-members of CCG. Before going any further I must recount a very small incident which nevertheless made a great impression on me. My room was cleaned by a woman who came in during the day and whom I never met. A day or so after I arrived I noticed a jar with some autumn flowers in it on my table. Flowers? The woman must have picked them in the waste land outside the building. A German woman and for me, whom she had never seen, a member of the occupying power? A kind of *collaboratrice* perhaps? Impossible. She didn't even know me. Just a friendly gesture it must have been. I wish the woman knew how my image of the Germans had been shaken.

There was a remarkable miscellany of men and women in the Control Commission for Germany. It seemed to me that nearly all of them fell into two main groups. The first was composed of individuals who, one could say, "wanted to do something about the Germans." Their aim, very broadly, was to influence, directly or indirectly, German public or private institutions such as schools, universities, newspapers, trade unions, professional associations and employers' federations in favour of more democratic and less authoritarian attitudes, in other words to counteract Nazism at source. It was an idealistic motivation. The second group comprised those who simply liked an easier job and a more comfortable life compared to anything which they might be able to get in the UK. Some of the latter, it is true, might have belonged to the first group in the early days of the occupation, when virtually all of the administration of the region was supervised by members of the CCG. As the Germans gradually took over, large numbers of the British became surplus to requirements and entered the second group before, often at quite a long interval, being finally declared redundant.

I have to say that, whatever purpose it may have served previously, by the time I joined Commerce Division it had become totally irrelevant to anything which was actually happening! Papers were busily passed from office to office of which the sole object seemed to be to keep their authors and readers occupied. To my inquiries about the business of Commerce Division I was informed, in the friendliest way, that this was a "policy-making body".

It was not long before I determined that I must get out of Commerce Division at any price. However, right at the beginning of my stay in Berlin I was given an interesting experience. I accompanied a senior official of the Division to a meeting of the representative of the four powers which each occupied a Sector of Berlin — British, US, French and Russian. The Agenda was composed of minor administrative matters which affected the city. Whenever one of the western Allies proposed something, no matter what, the Soviet representative simply said, "Nyet"! As all measures were supposed to be unanimous this amounted to a veto. After an hour or so, no action being possible, we all went in to rather a good meal!

My friend the Religious Affairs Adviser — his name was John Gwynne — visited Berlin after I had been there about two or three weeks. "You got me into this mess", I said to him, "and you must get me out of it." Somewhat amused, he said he would do what he could. In the meantime he introduced me to two remarkable women. They were respectively the wife and the sister of Peter Yorck von Wartemburg. Peter Yorck was a friend of Helmuth von Moltke and a member of the group which had tried to kill Hitler in what became known as the 20th of July (1944) plot. Yorke, Von Moltke and many others had been summarily tried and executed in the months that followed the plot.

It is a particularly sad point that Claus von Stauffenberg who actually placed the bomb on 20 July which almost, but not quite, killed Hitler, had made a previous attempt some weeks earlier. Apparently he had prepared a bomb which he had wrapped up, disguised as a bottle of cognac and asked a colleague, who was travelling with the Führer on his special plane, to pass it to one of his friends. The plane with Hitler and the bomb on board duly set off. To Stauffenberg's dismay, he received a message that Hitler had arrived at his destination without incident. He immediately took another plane (he was a senior staff officer), got hold of the colleague, told him that the bottle of cognac was the wrong one and handed over another parcel purporting to be the right one.

When he reached a place of safety, Stauffenberg opened the original parcel to find that the time-fuse had failed to fire the detonator. He had, so it seems, obtained his material from one of the SOE drops which had fallen into German hands. The fuse was known as a time pencil. This functioned by means of an acid set to eat through a wire in a given time. When the wire snapped a spring was activated which fired the detonator. In the course of SOE training we had been told that this mechanism was fallible and that we must always use two time pencils. (In the episode at the Le Mans Post Office we had actually used three.) Stauffenberg, of course, did not know about the precaution. If he had, the whole course of history might have been different. Obviously the bomb in the aeroplane would have been far more effective than the bomb in Stauffenberg's briefcase which later wounded Hitler, but failed to kill him.

Peter Yorck's widow was now working as a judge in Berlin. His sister was a doctor. Although I only knew these two women for a very short time, I think the fact that I had been a *resistant* enabled me to attain a community of spirit with them and indirectly with the conspirators of the 20th of July. I rapidly acquired a tremendous admiration for the courage and determination of this group of men and women. Many, but not all of them, belonged to the old German aristocracy and were devout Christians. They had become increasingly horrified at the crimes being committed by the all-powerful Nazi régime, notably by the SS and the Gestapo. It was their hope that, if only they could overthrow Hitler, the Allies might relent in demanding German total surrender and negotiate a peace with a non-Nazi government which had ousted him. As Marion Yorck said to me, "You cannot imagine how hard it is to hope that your own country will lose a war."

I was soon to hear a good deal about the German sense of duty (*Pflicht*). As it is certainly relevant to the history of the 20th of July plot, something must be said about it in this connection. There had been several German senior generals among the conspirators. These men might have helped in a *coup d'état* to topple the Nazi government if Hitler had been killed. As he was only wounded they felt that their oath of allegiance prevented them from such a revolutionary action. While they hesitated, events moved swiftly. The plot came to nothing, many brave and anti-Nazi Germans were executed and the Allies continued to demand total capitulation. They, nevertheless, showed that there was a different side to Germany than the crowds which had so ecstatically cheered the Führer at Nuremberg.

Every day I went to the office of Commerce Division I became so incensed at the uselessness of this body that, together, with two friends, I wrote a report which we sent to the Chief of Staff of the CCG, stating that in our opinion what we were supposed to being doing served no useful purpose whatsoever and requesting a change at the earliest possible opportunity. This damning document was received not unsympathetically by the head of the personnel department with whom we each had an interview. The short-term result was that the three of us were placed in a separate office, completely segregated from our fellows in Commerce Division — lest we contaminate them of course — and given absolutely nothing to do!

This state of affairs came to an end around the beginning of December '47 when I was informed that I was being transferred to Robert Birley's Education Department. He had a job which apparently involved looking after young miners. I was to be interviewed by the head of the Allied Coal Board and, if he approved of me, I was in. Apparently he did approve of me and then, when the various CCG formalities had been duly observed, I found myself on the Allied train out of Berlin bound for the Ruhr.

I arrived at Essen Hauptbahnkof on the bleakest December day imaginable. It was raining. There were no porters and no taxis. Laden with a large suitcase and a heavy kit-bag, I stood outside the station wondering what to do next. Eventually I noticed a sign and an arrow which seemed to indicate the way to some kind of CCG office; it led outside the station. There was nothing for it but to walk to wherever the arrows were leading, suitcase, kitbag and all. I passed under the railway and along a street in which every building had been destroyed. Eventually I came to the Bismarck Platz. The statue of the Iron Chancellor was still standing defiantly in the middle of the Square, although there were many holes and dents in the bronze. At the side of the Square was a large building which seemed to have been patched up. In it was housed a signals unit of the CCG. They came to my rescue with one of their trucks. I soon found myself comfortably housed, but how was I to get on with my task of looking after young miners? A day or two after my arrival an embarrassing incident took place in the CCG mess in which I was quartered which highlighted my problem. A man asked me what my job was. On my replying that I was charged with organizing the welfare of young miners he said, "I suppose it is your experience of Germany that led you to this job?" I confessed to knowing nothing about Germany. "Your knowledge of youth work must be your background." Uncomfortably I disclaimed any knowledge of youth work. "Ah. Of course you will have had a career in the mining industry?" he pursued. It was too much, getting quickly to my feet, I explained that I must go to an urgent meeting. Thanking him for the interesting conversation I rapidly departed!

Fortunately, before trying to get into my job, I had asked the CCG to arrange a visit for me to the British coal mines and welfare institutions. It was actually set up by the Miners' Welfare Commission and was certainly quite instructive. After a week or two meeting Welfare Officers and members of various committees, I returned to Germany with at least some ideas as to how I might tackle the task which lay before me. I was allocated an office in the building occupied by the German Coal Mines Organization (DKBL) and an English-speaking secretary. My German was still very elementary, but now, under pressure, began to improve fast, though perhaps without too much concern for grammar or the gender of nouns!

My first step was to procure the preparation of a rubber stamp bearing the inscription, in English "Miners' Welfare Organization." From my days in the Sarthe I knew how impressed the Germans could be with any form of rubber stamp. That the inscription was in English gave it the aura of the Allied occupation — still a potent factor in those days!

I visited a number of the so-called "camps" for young miners and was appalled at the conditions they were living under. Of course, the cities of the Ruhr were areas of total devastation, with the inhabitants living mainly in the cellars of their houses so that the managers of the mines could hardly be expected to give priority in matters of comfort to able-bodied young men. Even so, some action seemed very much to be called for. I had formed a number of useful contacts amongst the top officials of the DKBL and without much difficulty persuaded them (in those days CCG still had some authority!) to set up a Welfare Commission, rather on the model of the British one. It was termed the "*Kommission für Soziale Aufgaben im Kohlenbergbau*".

In order to get to know the situation better, I decided to live in one of the camps for young miners for a week and try actually working underground. It was an interesting experience. I developed a respect for miners which has lasted ever since. The often cramped conditions, the dust and, above all, the amount of physical effort needed in the work seemed to make any surface job relatively easy. Of course Germany in 1947 was not an easy life for anybody. Rations were so meagre that somehow they had to be supplemented by what could be had on the black market. Employers often paid wages and salaries in kind. Miners were given probably better rations than most of the population, but even that did not amount to much. One extraordinary addition to the miners' pay, even the youngest among them, was a monthly allocation of two bottles of schnapps (about 40% alcohol content). It was the custom to trade one for any other useful articles that might be available and keep one for a monthly booze-up. I was glad not be in the camp when the allocation was given out!

During this time I saw little of my fellow members of CCG. With few exceptions, they appeared to live in a world apart. Increasingly the German administration was being reborn and where the expatriates had probably contributed usefully to the resuscitation of German industry they were now increasingly surplus to anything that was needed.

The reader may be surprised that in the preceding chapters I have said nothing about my encounters with Nazis. In fact I was surprised that in all my time in Germany I didn't encounter any! Not quite true. One personable young man whom I met during my underground experience claimed to have been a Nazi. The only one! Almost the entire population appeared to have undergone a remarkable rationalization process, partly unconscious, partly conscious. It ran, more or less, as follows in individual terms:

- I did not like the Nazis. If I were a party member, it was only because of my job, my friends, etc.
- I joined the Army, the Hitlerjugend, the Bund Deutscher Madchen, etc., etc. because everybody else was in it and in any case I was obliged to sign up.
- I didn't know anything about the concentration camps or the extermination policy towards Jews.
- I sometimes thought that the Nazis were wrong, but I felt it was my duty to obey.

The attitude of the Germans towards any kind of authority was not to be understood by the democratic societies of the west. Before the days of Hitler and the Nazis, there must have been a strong authoritarian trend running through German society as a whole — respect for one's parents, teachers and pastor or priest, virtuous in itself, but dangerous if carried to extremes. Adults carried this attitude over in their relationship to employers and managers, military officers, officials and civil servants and, of course, the Government. Just to make sure that these attitudes were maintained the Nazis installed a system of "*Blockleiter*" (house block supervisors) and then there was the Gestapo with its elaborate network of informers and its means of extracting information from all but the most heroic.

"I considered it my duty as a soldier, to obey orders to the end." How else is it possible to explain that, although the war was manifestly lost from the time the Allies broke through on the Normandy front, the Germans continued to put up such a desperate resistance? The demoralized German soldiers we had witnessed streaming from the Falaise Pocket in August 1944 had somehow been brought under control, even to the point of mounting the Ardennes Offensive of December '44 and blowing up the Rhine bridges in April '45.

What had obviously been an all-pervading admiration, even adoration, of the Führer had, in appearance, totally vanished. With defeat, the idol had not only been revealed as having feet of clay, but had been brought crashing down and smashed itself in the process. So it was on the surface, but who could know what psychological traumas might be hidden underneath the smiling faces of the Germans I was working with from day to day?

Then, of course, there was the "victory factor". When Hitler's armies were crushing all opposition from the

Pyrenees to Moscow how could any patriotic German restrain his or her pride? Prostrate under the Treaty of Versailles, then resurgent as the Führer's all-conquering *Herrenvolk*. Now the world had collapsed about them again. We, the Allies, and more especially the British, were now entitled to the respect which was the victor's due in a society brought up on military prowess.

Another extremely important component of what may, perhaps, be termed the German "collective psyche" is compulsion to work. To some extent this is true of many western societies, particularly those where the so-called "protestant ethic" insists that a man must have a job to ensure his self-respect. However, nowhere was this more the case than in Germany. This deification of work was a most powerful element in Hitler's rise to power. In the terrible unemployment of the twenties and thirties, Hitler had held out the prospect of a job for everyone and in the Third Reich this promise was fulfilled. No unemployment there!

With the collapse of the economy after the defeat of 1945 everyone was living hand-to-mouth.

In July 1948 an event of major historical significance took place. This was the total and drastic reform of the German currency. Reichmarks vanished and were replaced by Deutsch-marks. This was an Allied initiative applicable to the three western zones of occupation. It coincided with the immediate arrival of what was called Marshall Aid, the scheme initiated by US Secretary of State, General George Marshall. This supplied to the market large quantities of consumer goods. The effect was instantaneous and had to be seen to be believed. Gone were the days of the black market, of wages paid in kind and of town-dwellers making excursions into the countryside to swap their household belongings for the farmers' ham and butter. It was a joke at the time that the farmers were running out of space in their barns to hang the carpets which the townspeople were trading in for butter.

All of this ended with the currency reform. Every man and woman could now work for proper wages. German industry was on its way to the *Wirschaftwunder*, the economic miracle.

Coal production in the mines of the Ruhr rose steadily and rapidly. Steel production which had been limited to a ceiling by the Allies now began to exceed the limit — with the result that the limit was taken away! Another result of the *Wunder* was the sudden complete availability of every kind of eatable. This may partly have been the result of Marshall Aid imports and partly because the German farmers, now able to sell their produce for the new "hard" D-mark, were happy to put an end to all rationing. One curious effect was that nearly all individuals, men and women, put on weight by leaps and bounds. I could hardly recognize some of my friends and acquaintances after two to three months.

All of this might never have happened, or in a process maybe lasting for years, if it had not been for the most sudden reversal of national policy in all of history. Our gallant ally against Germany, the Union of Soviet Socialist Republics led by friendly old Uncle Joe, was suddenly seen to be the most dangerous enemy of the western democracies. Churchill's famous speech in which he described Europe as being divided by an *Iron Curtain* stretching across all of Germany was the start which initiated this far-reaching change of attitude. The effect on the policy of the occupiers of the British, American and French zones of Germany was dramatic. I may list the changeover as follows:

BEFORE

We must eliminate all elements of Nazism.

Those who had been in positions of authority in Hitlerian times must not be allowed to attain such positions again.

German industry must be severely limited in scope and levels of production.

The German population must, of course, have enough food, but otherwise there should be no great concern about raising the standard of living.

Trade Unions were to be encouraged to counteract the overdominant influence of employers.

AFTER

Except for the most prominent war criminals, ex-Nazis could be tolerated and even permitted to occupy positions of influence. Everything should be done to further the economic recovery of the country as a counter-measure to Communist influence in the Soviet zone of occupation.

Industry should be encouraged to increase production without limitation.

Trade Unions should collaborate with employers in the recovery of industry.

In short, a resurgent Western Germany should be a bulwark against the Soviet power in Europe and particularly its menacing presence in the Eastern Zone.

This very short summary is only intended to illustrate the remarkable change in the situation in which the Control Commission found itself. Its staff now began to be steadily made redundant. Here again was a phenomenon. The CCG members who were most professionally qualified started to leave of their own accord. The less able stayed on as long as they could. The Germans now began rapidly to "do things on their own" and made a rather good job of their reviving industry. The blast furnaces of Muelheim, Rheinhausen and Bochum made the sky over the cities glow at night. Too bad that more than a few of the directors and managers were in the same positions they had occupied under the Nazis!

I will not bore my readers with any detailed account of my activities during the period from 1948 to 1952. I continued my employment with CCG until my contract came to an end in 1951 and then worked on a series of short-term assignments for the U.S. High Commission for Germany (HICOG) for approximately two years. Most of the time I spent with the U.S. High Commission was in Baden-Würtemberg, although I spent several months in the Ruhr. My job was in the general fields of Industrial Relations and Welfare in Industry — what would now be termed Human Resources. The work, together with that of my British, American and German colleagues, involved seminars, study visits to Britain and America, attitude surveys and the setting up of various institutions. I was also involved in different aspects of adult education. Incredibly I even represented Germany at a UNESCO meeting in Florence in 1952! While there, I argued strongly in favour of the establishment of a UNESCO social research institute in Germany. (It actually was established.) However, although fascinating, the whole experience left me somewhat disillusioned with UNESCO. It seemed that its lofty objectives were hard to reconcile with the sometimes irrelevant arguments and the jockeying for position which often characterized its debates.

It was during 1952 that my wife Joan, who was now living permanently in Switzerland, agreed to a divorce. I had thought that I would experience a sense of liberation. Instead I just felt sad. I did not feel a sense of guilt. Was it my fault that the man whom Joan had married in Switzerland so many years ago had, over the intervening period, become a different personality?

The reason why I do not intend to bore my readers with more information about my activities during this period is simply because the great majority of our efforts, including those which accomplished something and those which did not, have now vanished into oblivion. This is not to say that they were purposeless at the time, just that they have been absorbed into the general current of German history. However, three situations in which I was involved as a participant or as a spectator may be of interest.

The years following the currency reform not only saw an immense resurgence of German industry, they also marked a remarkable development of Trade Union power. Co-determination (*Mitbestimmungsrecht*) was a plan which Trade Union leaders had prepared during the Nazi domination, while they were in prison, in hiding or abroad. I may summarize very briefly the way in which it was applied in the Coal and Steel industries of the Ruhr. Each company consisted of a Supervisory Board composed of equal numbers of employer-nominated members and Trade Union-nominated members. The chairman was supposedly neutral. Responsible to the Supervisory Board was the Executive Board with three members, of which the "Labour Director" (in present day parlance the Human Resources Director) was nominated by the Trade Union.

In the non-coal and steel industries the Supervisory Board contained only one-third Trade Union nominees and the executive in charge of Human Resources was not a Trade Union nominee. When the legislation containing the co-determination laws came into force around 1950, my friends among the employers were in despair, those amongst the Trade Unionists were triumphant.

Six months later the picture had changed in a way which had to be seen to be believed. Many stalwart

Trade Unionists, men who had suffered for their convictions under the Nazis, were now Labour Directors. They rapidly became more employer-minded than the other directors. There can be little doubt that the latter, even if they did not deliberately set out to corrupt the Labour Director, at least made sure that he had a more than comfortable office with all the trimmings. I may cite one example, out of many, of how the system influenced the attitudes of those who directly participated in it.

I was one day visiting the Labour Director of one of the Ruhr's major steel works. He was a man who had been imprisoned under the Nazis and emerged as one of the founders of the new German Trade Union movement (much encouraged by the Western Allies as what they regarded as a counterweight to any Nazi-minded employers). I drove into the plant and asked a man in overalls where the office of the *Herr Arbeitsdirector* might be situated.

"Ach", said the man, "that's *drei-liter* Willi."

"*Drei-liter* Willi?" I questioned, in considerable astonishment. He explained that the Labour Director was so-called in the plant as he had been allocated the first three litre Mercedes to be purchased for the company's transport fleet! I proceeded to the very large luxurious office of the Labour Director. As an obsequious secretary poured coffee for us he explained that the disciplining of "our" workforce needed to be tightened up. "And," he added, "I made sure that the branch secretary of the Union agreed with me!"

There were many stories such as this. The American Trade Unionists working on the HICOG staff were particularly horrified at their colleagues' blatant collusion with the employers. However, it had to be admitted that the system really worked in a remarkable way. The German unions did actively collaborate with the employers' organizations to ensure a long period of industrial peace. This effectively put German manufacturing in the lead among its European competitors.

Towards the end of 1953 I became involved in a series of experimental seminars for young Germans who had managed to escape from the DDR (the Russian zone of occupation). By 1953 any crossing of the line of demarcation between East and West Germany had become an extremely hazardous undertaking. The Berlin Wall and lines of guard-posts, electrified fences and barbed wire stretched from the North Sea to the Austrian frontier. Small numbers of people were sometimes permitted to visit their relations in the West, but such authorizations were few and far between. However, one way or another, some young people got across. They were motivated by a feeling that life in the West would give them greatly enhanced opportunities, freedom from the stiflingly repressive régime of the Communist party and, of course, the streets of the cities of Western Germany were paved with gold, weren't they?!

Experience had shown that many of the young people found it much more difficult to adapt to life in western society than they had expected. Under the Communist régime of the East every step of your life was directed for you. There was no choice. You might not like your job, but you always had one. It was cradle-to-grave paternalism, or, more correctly perhaps, despotism. For individuals accustomed to the way of life of the DDR it was a shock to find that they had to seek a job for themselves. In fact the Federal Republic, with a steadily increasing level of prosperity, did provide many services for its citizens. The difficulty was in knowing where to go, to what office of what particular service one should apply. All so different from the East. Small wonder that many of the ex-Easterners became disillusioned and sometimes even managed to return to the régime from which they had fled. Matters were not improved by the reception centres established by the West German regional authorities through which all persons coming from the DDR were obliged to pass in order to check their identity and provide them with new papers.

Our seminars were of two weeks' duration and designed to promote as much free discussion as possible — something to which no one from the East Zone was accustomed. Otherwise the programme was directed to the task of adapting to the Western way of life, in particular job finding. The seminars were, at the time, quite a success, perhaps not so much due to the programme content but more as to the evident interest and concern with which the young people were treated by their tutors.

Very occasionally over the years, even though I was actually employed by the British and American Commissions, the question occurred to me, was I becoming too "Germanized"? I seemed to be identifying myself with the Germans in the same way that I had once identified with the French in their underground struggle against the Germans. I sometimes felt twinges of conscience at this transformation. I rationalized it to myself that all of it was in the cause of a new Germany, repudiating the Nazi past, and fitting itself for integration into, what we might hope, would be a new Europe. It may be that history has not recognized what the CCG and its companion organizations in the American and French zones of occupation did accomplish in what was known at the time as the "re-orientation of Germany". Did we not perhaps contribute something in the crucial years, when Germany was struggling to find a new direction after Nazism's total defeat, to the reconstruction of a nation which was to evolve into the leading democracy of Europe?

I mentioned earlier another project with which I was particularly concerned. Throughout my years in the Ruhr I had been involved in several projects connected with the Institute for Social Research of the University of Munster, located in Dortmund. About the middle of 1952, with a number of British, American and German friends, I became interested in establishing a conference centre under the auspices of the University which would, in the main, be dedicated to meetings and seminars covering management-employee relations and subjects relating to Adult Education in industrial areas. Nothing came of this idea until the American

High Commission agreed to produce the necessary funding. Needless to say, matters proceeded quite fast from this point. A member of the Institute for Social Research was nominated as Director, a large and pleasant house about 10 kms south of Dortmund was rented, domestic staff was engaged and the programme went ahead more or less as planned. Quite a number of influential people in the Ruhr became interested. Some of the seminars were entirely German, others had a sprinkling of British, Americans and French. Quite a few comprised young men (they were mostly men) who, it was thought would benefit from the international atmosphere which it had been one of the objects of the Centre to create. There were also study groups composed of managers, members of works councils and academics, usually about twelve to fifteen individuals in each. Most of the seminars, which lasted one or two weeks, were residential except for visiting lecturers and discussion leaders. The Conference Centre was officially registered as "Haus Ahlenberg" with the city of Dortmund and given the status of a training centre for adults.

When the conference centre had been operational for some six months it was decided to appoint a person who would manage its finances while at the same time acting as host or hostess to the various groups and the international assortment of speakers and visitors. I thought I knew someone who might prove an ideal choice. Fraülein Ruth Risse was the librarian to the Coal Control Headquarters of the CCG and had also been responsible for a number of other administrative tasks. It was clear that the Coal Control was now totally surplus to any requirements. Indeed many of its staff had already left Germany and it was obvious that it would shortly be wound up altogether. Fraülein Risse would surely be looking for a new job and I approached her with an offer of a position of Manager/Hostess at Haus Ahlenberg. After some hesitation she decided to accept it. We were all extremely pleased. Not only was Fraulein Risse an exceedingly good-looking young woman — she was aged about thirty — but was possessed of a singularly radiant personality which ensured that she was universally popular. Little by little I got to know her background. It is a story which I will recount, not only for its intrinsic tragic interest, but because it illustrates the darkest side of recent German history, the side of which so much had remained hidden in the post-war period.

I have mentioned before that I felt I might be becoming too German-orientated. The Germans with whom I worked on so many projects were invariably friendly and co-operative. They appeared unanimous in disliking Hitler and the Nazi régime and were always careful to explain that their efforts in the armed services, in the civil service or in industrial manufacturing, were simply in the cause of duty. I knew, of course, about the Concentration Camps, Auschwitz, Oradour sur Glane and so many other atrocities. Well, perhaps these could be attributed to Hitler himself, to Himmler, to the SS, to the Gestapo and to their collaborators. However, in newsreels I had seen the Nürnberg rallies and the crowds lining the streets to cheer the Führer with innumerable flags emblazoned with the swastika floating from the windows of the houses. I knew all these events as a matter of history, but I did not have any direct human experience of them. The case of the family of Fraülein Risse gave me a new insight into German society and its all-pervading evil during the Nazi years from 1933 to 1945.

This was the way it happened.

Emil Risse was born a Catholic. However, in the year immediately following the First World War he met and married a girl from a Jewish family, Julia Salomon. Neither of them actually practised their religion. They had a son Rolf and a daughter Ruth. Emil had a small but quite prosperous business and the family lived contentedly in Essen during the years until 1933 when Adolf Hitler became Chancellor of Germany.

For many the writing was on the wall. Jewish families began to emigrate to America, to Britain, to France, anywhere outside what was now becoming the Third Reich. After the *Kristallnacht* in 1938, the night in which the windows of Jewish shops were smashed by Nazi mobs, the anti-Jewish policy at the highest level of the Nazi party and the Government became devastatingly clear and, while the frontiers remained open, Jewish emigration became a flood.

Herr Risse, however, would not move. He had no friends or relations abroad and he had his business to consider. His wife had been converted to the Evangelical Church. The children went through school and, near the beginning of the war, completed the Abitur. Frau Risse did not go out, except in the immediate neighbourhood of her home, and Herr Risse continued in his business.

In 1939 Rolf was called up for military service. He appeared very smart in his new uniform, a swastika on his armband and, incredible as it may seem, both he and his mother were quite proud of his military appearance. It was not to last long. The authorities of the Wehrmacht discovered Rolf's half-Jewish antecedents and he was discharged from the Army. This apparently came as a terrible blow to his self-esteem; all his friends of his own age group were now in the armed services. His personality was severely traumatized.

Ruth served a six-month spell in the *Arbeitsdienst*, doing farm work and returned with an offer to stay on as a group leader, an offer which she declined. The family lived on relatively undisturbed until March 1943.

I was in the *Maison Central d'Eysses* at that time and I well remember one of the warders whispering to me, "*Mille bombardiers sur Essen*". It was indeed one of the first of the thousand-bomber raids. A torrent of firebombs and high explosives descended upon Essen. Within the hour Herr Risse was contemplating the destruction of his house and everything it contained. The family had managed to escape before their home was smashed and they were fortunate in obtaining a flat in one of the suburbs of the city. The air-raids were continually increasing in severity — the RAF by night and the USAAF by day — and the Esseners were obliged to make increasing use of the air-raid shelters. Frau Risse, although converted to Christianity, was nevertheless considered Jewish and was not allowed to use the public shelters. She was obliged to remain in the house and her daughter stayed with her throughout the bombing.

It was Ruth, the daughter, who, at Christmas 1943, accompanied by a woman living in a nearby flat, went to a Roman Catholic midnight Mass. They returned without there being any air-raid. The war was approaching a climax in 1944. On 6 June the Allies had landed in Normandy and by October they were attacking the frontiers of the Reich. The Russians in the East were now driving the German armies steadily before them. It should have been evident to everyone that Nazi Germany was defeated. One would have imagined that Frau Risse, who had survived unmolested for so long, when so many Jews had been transported to the Concentration Camps, would now be approaching a situation of increasing safety.

One night the Gestapo knocked on the door. They had come to arrest Frau Risse They explained that the very neighbour with whom the daughter had gone to midnight Mass had denounced Frau Risse as Jewish. They took her away to the Gestapo prison in Essen. She remained there in the winter of 1944-45. Surprisingly, one of the warders approached Frau Risse and offered to let her escape through the cellars of the building. However, on hearing that there might be reprisals against her family she refused the offer. She does not seem to have been treated with any brutality and her daughter was allowed to visit her from time to time.

In the spring of 1945 there were about 250 prisoners in the Gestapo's Essen Prison. The Americans had now crossed the Rhine at Remagen and the British north of Duisberg. Their armies were rapidly surrounding the Ruhr area with a pincer movement. The Gestapo chief, an SS officer, Betz by name, decided to evacuate the prisoners through the rapidly narrowing gap to the east. Unknown to any of their families and friends, the prisoners were loaded into trucks for the journey. They proceeded in convoy some way beyond Dortmund when Betz realized that the gap was already closed. He made the prisoners get out of the trucks and marched them into a field. Then, unbelievably, he ordered the Gestapo guards to shoot them all. Thus perished Frau Julia Risse, a victim of Nazi Germany. The situation was made even more agonizing for Frau Risse's family by the fact that they had absolutely no knowledge of what had become of her. They hoped against hope that she had somehow survived and would return to them. Only as the months went by were they forced to accept the bitter truth.

It seems incredible that Betz did not simply hand his prisoners over to the Allies, in which case he would certainly have saved his own skin. As it was, he escaped capture for some time, was finally apprehended and hanged himself in his cell while awaiting trial in Wuppertal. The neighbour who denounced Frau Risse to the Gestapo, on the arrival of the Allied troops in Essen, fled to the Eastern Zone, leaving her flat and most of her possessions behind her.

I have recounted this terrible series of events partly because I was in direct contact with the surviving family and partly because they seem to exemplify, in microcosm, the way in which Nazism destroyed all sense of humanity.

If Herr Risse had left Germany in 1933–34, of course, all would have been well. But why should he? He was a good German citizen and would always maintain that "we did nothing wrong". How could he know until it was too late that the authority of the State, which should have been his protector, was implacably turned against him and his family? The denunciation of Frau Risse to the Gestapo by the neighbour and Betz's order to massacre his prisoners appears to be Nazism in its very essence of evil.

Many years after these events took place Frau Risse's granddaughter, then an attractive young woman in her twenties named Karen, asked me how it was possible for the Germans to have committed such inhuman crimes. Certainly my answer to her question was lamentably inadequate. It is a question which I have often thought about. Surely there must be some answer. Perhaps there were several causes which contributed to the terrible phenomenon, that in the words of Jean-Paul Sartre's anti-hero "the reign of evil has begun upon the earth".

May it be that the psychopathic roots of the Nazi system of beliefs lie in what maybe termed the "urge for power"? In an authoritarian society, such as that which long prevailed in Germany, it may be argued that the latent resentment in having to submit to superiors engenders a desire to oppress those in a position of inferiority to oneself. The exploitation of this trait could well have been an important factor in the Nazis' rise to the domination of German society. Thus men whose abilities would have limited them to relatively subordinate positions now found themselves with the power to put their fellow citizens in prison or even to determine matters of life and death — for example the Blockleiter and Kreisleiter, officials of the various organizations of the Nazi party, members of the SS, concentration camp warders and of course the Secret State Police, the Gestapo.

This factor, though perhaps contributing to individual motivations, was surely not the only cause of the horrors perpetrated by the Nazis. Theirs was a system which drew on the darker side of the human ego.

It would seem that in the complex psychology of the nature of man there is an elemental urge for cruelty as well as a corresponding urge for compassion. Under the Nazi régime the former urge was exploited by an endless stream of propaganda. This was diverted towards creating, one may say, an atmosphere combining exhilaration with fear; exhilaration at a sense of participation in the triumphs of the Third Reich; fear of being denounced for reasons of jealousy or pure malice by a network of informers leading to arrest by the Gestapo.

Thus the German population was powerfully induced to believe that:

- Adolf Hitler was destined to be the creator and supreme Führer of the Third Reich and all who were empowered by him, directly or indirectly, must be obeyed without question.
- The Germans were the supreme race of mankind, both culturally and militarily.
- All weaker nations were deserving of contempt and should be subordinate to the *Herrenvolk*.
- The Jews were selected as an object on which hatred could be focused. (That many Jews had served bravely in the German Army in the First World War was obliterated from the collective memory.)
- All resistance to the Nazi régime was punishable by imprisonment or death. (Even listening to foreign broadcasts was subject to severe penalties.)
- The holding of hostages was a recognized means of ensuring compliance with Nazi objectives.
- Above all the national sense of duty, probably dating back to the time of Frederick the Great, was exploited to the limit. "I had to do my duty" was an excuse for innumerable crimes as well as for acts of bravery in the field.

At the beginning of this book the ethical question was raised as to whether, in the face of Nazi aggression, the man or woman of true virtue should declare him, or her, self to be pacifist and renounce all participation in war. Many philosophers, including Plato and Epictetus, have held the view that ignorance is the cause of evil and that if an individual intending to commit an evil deed could be shown the way to a more virtuous course of action he would surely follow it. It would certainly seem in retrospect that no amount of philosophical reasoning or Christian "turning the other cheek" or Buddhist "compassion for all sentient beings" or Gandhian doctrine of "non-violence" would have had the slightest impact on the devotees of the National Socialist state, no matter whether these were at the pinnacle of authority or totally subordinate. In his book *Mein Kampf* Adolf Hitler had expressed with devastating clarity the creed of total combat, stating, "He who would live must fight. He who does not wish to fight in this world, where permanent struggle is the law of life, has not the right to exist."

At this point we may recall the way in which Noor and Vilayet Inayat Khan dealt with the question. Their father had been the founder of Sufism in the West and the two had been brought up on a philosophy of absolute pacifism. In 1939 they were faced with the agonizing choice — pacifism or participation in the war. They finally decided that Nazism was so evil that it must be confronted at all costs and that they should volunteer for frontline service in the Forces. Vilayet joined the minesweepers of the Royal Navy. Noor became an SOE F Section radio operator in German-occupied France. After a time she was pinpointed by the German tracking service and shot. She was posthumously awarded the George Cross. Her brother survived the war and became a teacher of Sufi philosophy.

We may perhaps leave this momentous and disturbing ethical dilemma by quoting Epictetus, "If evil men appear thou wilt clear the earth of them." "But if I die thus?" "Thou wilt die a good man in the accomplishing of a noble deed."

May all those who sacrificed their lives in the struggle against the evil of the Third Reich be long remembered.

CHAPTER FOURTEEN

Return To "Normal" Life

Haus Ahlenberg marked the end of my activities in Germany. It was now mid-1953, the economic miracle was in full swing and it was evident that all Allied-sponsored schemes, whatever value they may have had, were beginning to look increasingly anachronistic as far as I was concerned. My six years in Germany had certainly helped me, should I say recover, from my destabilizing experiences in SOE. Although I had no illusions as to how much I had accomplished, at least I probably helped some German institutions and individuals in adjusting to the better values of the Western world after their experiences of Nazism and of war. My own ambition for a more idealistic way of life than selling chemicals in Switzerland had been partially satisfied. Perhaps, I thought at the time, this curious non-egoism might have gone too far. I was surprised by one of the participants in an Ahlenberg Seminar saying to me, "You are a very interesting man. I have noticed that you obtain all your satisfaction in life through the activities of other people." If this were really true, it would be a philosophical objective one might think. Nevertheless there seemed to be something slightly unhealthy about such an attitude. Certainly in the world in which I would now have to make my way something rather more positive would surely be required.

I returned to London, my first thought being to try to find employment in some international agency or other. I soon realized that during my long stay in Germany most, if not all, interesting positions had long been taken. I was obliged to seek a job elsewhere. Fortunately, through an influential friend and supported by Maurice Buckmaster, my one time chief of SOE F Section, I was offered a job in Shell as what would now be termed Manager of Human Resources. My job was to be in Israel, well paid, interesting and with an assured future. What more could anybody want? It was not perhaps the "do-gooder" agency which I had first thought of. However, it was a job with some social content nonetheless. In short, I supposed I had in some measure re-adapted myself to normal life. Before going out to Israel, Ruth Risse and I were married in May 1954.

In joining Shell I entered a new world. How secure it was and yet how restricted compared to the dozen years which had gone before. Whatever else they had done for me, I had certainly learned a lot about human nature!

Post-War Careers

It may be interesting to outline briefly what I know of the postwar history of the principal persons who figure in my autobiography. I will list them more or less in the chronological order in which they appear in the text.

France

Brian Rafferty was executed in Flossenberg on 29 March 1944.

George Jones continued to live in Paris and became a Thomas Cook Tour Guide, showing tourists around the capital.

Roger Werther, my particular friend and cell companion, was transferred from SOE to the French Army and not long after was killed in an accident.

Madame Werther returned to Passy, re-occupied her shop there and later retired.

Yvan Gaillard, the prison warder who largely contributed to our escape from Eysses, came with us to the Pyrenees, joined F Section and after training was parachuted into France. After the war he went back to his job as warder. Interestingly, although sadly, he was not promoted to *surveillant-chef* until near the end of his career. Evidently his superiors did not approve of his joining SOE and the French Resistance.

Andre Lescorat was, for some time, Mayor of Villeneuve sur Lot.

Robert Bruhl, ex-*Maison Centrale*, became a Colonel in the Engineers' Corps of the French Army.

Danielle and her husband, who sheltered us for three days at the foot of the Pyrenees, somehow survived the war.

Angel, the *passeur* and our guide through the Pyrenees, was murdered by some of his fellow smugglers in 1944.

Philippe de Vômecourt ran a large Resistance organisation in Central France. After the war he established himself in business.

Edmond Cohin sold the Château des Bordeaux and became something of a recluse.

Pierre-Raimond Glaesner, ex-*Maison Centrale* and SOE. Joined the French Army.

Sonia and Guy d'Artois. Guy became a professional officer in the Canadian Army. They had six children.

The brothers Hillaret. Two survived the war.

Abbe Chevalier became Bishop of Le Mans.

Thailand

Chin (Prince Svasti) lived for a time in the UK and then returned to Bangkok.

Nicky (I never knew his real name) became fed up with the Royal life in Thailand and, I believe, settled down in the UK.

Chew (Snoh Nilkamhaeng) pursued a business career in Bangkok.

Alex Griswold returned to a major financial organization in the US.

Luang Pradit (Pridi Panomyong) gradually lost power and emigrated (or was exiled) to Peiping.

Philip Toosey rejoined Barings in the City. (He was said to be extremely annoyed with the film *The Bridge on the River Kwai*, where he was depicted as Colonel Nicholson, collaborating with the Japanese in endeavouring to save the Bridge!)

Chris Blathwayte joined a firm of Chartered Accountants in the West of England.

David Smiley became a Colonel in the Guards.

It seems difficult to draw any definite conclusion from the brief synopses of the careers subsequent to the Second World War of the persons who have figured in my book. Certainly many of them did not find it easy to return to civilian life. Nevertheless, they did succeed in integrating themselves, more or less, in a way of life similar to that which they had led in pre-war days. The need to earn a living was, of course, an important factor in the lives of most of them. It does, however, seem curious that the motivation which led them to volunteer for, one may say, rather a risky and particularly lonely type of job in wartime did not appear to have urged them to any particularly altruistic course of conduct when the war was over.

Could it be that the men and women, coming from many different backgrounds and walks of life alike only in their knowledge of a foreign language, were drawn by the stimulating excitement of the undercover war and then reverted, not without some difficulty, to the type of existence to which they had been previously accustomed. There were exceptions of course. I have to admit to being one of them.

The Basic Principles of Underground Warfare 1942–45

Define your objectives. Be realistic. Don't "bite off more than you can chew" with the resources available.

Never get in a position where guerrillas confront trained army units. Strike, then disappear.

Make sure that your HQ or leader/s do not get caught. If he/she/they remain intact the organization can always grow again.

Adopt the principle of "cells". These should be unconnected with each other except through contact with the leader of the organization. Even the leadership had best not know where the individual members are living.

Use the smallest group possible to achieve your objective.

Assure your line of retreat or escape.

Women may be better agents than men and certainly less liable to arouse suspicion. A man together with a woman will also attract less notice than a man alone.

Strategy must be adapted to the particular type of area, e.g. hidden agents, Maquis, Chindits or some combination of the three.

If you want to conceal something, don't swear anybody/everybody to silence. Tell as many other stories as possible!

If someone gets caught he/she should have a "reserve cover story". At worst he/she must hold out for 24 hours so as to give time to other people "in the know" to make themselves scarce!

Never put anything in writing unless it is absolutely necessary. If you must, when it has served its purpose — destroy it.

The Qualities of Leadership — An Outline

Leadership is fundamentally the ability to influence others in such a way that they may share one's objectives and follow a course of action, which may lead to the fulfilment of those objectives.

Leaders have been virtuous or evil. It may be that they have a number of common attributes, such as:-

1. An unshakeable belief in the value of one's objectives.
2. A sense of mission. The ability to communicate this sense to others.
3. The ability to formulate ideas, verbally and in writing.
4. A "helicopter" view; the ability to view situations "from above", taking full cognisance of all contributing factors.

5. A conscious projection of one's own personality according to the requirements of any given background.

6. A distance, however slight or however great, from those which it is one's intent to lead.

7. The ability to control and, on occasion, to conceal one's own emotions.

8. The ability to arouse the emotions of others and to give them a desired direction.

9. A confidence in one's own ability to carry the mission, whether internally or externally imposed.

10. The ability to get a good night's sleep in the most adverse circumstances!

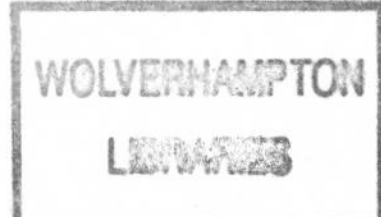